PURITAN PAPERBACKS

Preparations for Sufferings

John Flavel

c. 1630–1691

John Flavel, son of a Puritan minister who died in prison for his Nonconformity, was educated at University College, Oxford, and laboured for almost the entire period of his ministry at Dartmouth, Devon. Having all the characteristics of the tradition to which he belonged – a tradition which believed that preaching should be 'hissing hot,' searching and expository – Flavel attained to pre-eminence in his ability to combine both instruction and an appeal to the heart. Some Puritans might be more learned than he, and some more quaint, but for all-round usefulness none was his superior. The repeated editions of Flavel's writings bear witness to his popularity. He is one of that small number of evangelical writers who can by their lucidity and simplicity help those at the beginning of the Christian life and at the same time be a strong companion to those near its end.

John Flavel

Preparations for Sufferings

or

The Best Work in the Worst Times

*Wherein the Necessity, Excellency, and Means of
Our Readiness for Sufferings Are Evinced and
Prescribed; our Call to Suffering Cleared,
and the Great Unreadiness of Many
Professors Bewailed.*

THE BANNER OF TRUTH TRUST

THE BANNER OF TRUTH TRUST

Head Office
3 Murrayfield Road
Edinburgh, EH12 6EL
UK

North America Office
PO Box 621
Carlisle, PA 17013
USA

banneroftruth.org

Preparations for Sufferings first published London, 1682
The text of this edition is based on
The Works of John Flavel, vol. 6
(1820, repr. London: Banner of Truth Trust, 1968)
The Banner of Truth Trust © 2021

*

ISBN
Print: 978 1 80040 067 2
Epub: 978 1 80040 068 9
Kindle: 978 1 80040 069 6

*

Typeset in 10/13 Minion Pro at
The Banner of Truth Trust, Edinburgh

Printed in the USA by
Versa Press Inc.,
East Peoria, IL.

Contents

The Epistle to the Reader

It was the observation of the learned Gerson (when the world was not so old by many years as now it is) that *mundus senescens patitur phantasias:*[1] The aged world, like aged persons, dotes and grows whimsical, in its old age; the truth of which observation is confirmed by no one thing more, than the fond and groundless dreams and phantasms of tranquillity, and continuing prosperity, wherewith the multitude please themselves, even whilst the sins of the times are so great, and the signs of the times so sad and lowring as they are.

It is not the design of this *Manual* to scare and affright any man with imaginary dangers, much less to sow jealousies, and foment the discontents of the times; it being a just matter of lamentation that all the tokens of God's anger produce with many of us no better fruit but bold censures and loud clamours, instead of humiliation for our own sins, and the due preparation to take up our own cross, and follow Christ in a suffering path, which is the only mark and aim of this tract.

We read the histories of the primitive sufferers, but not with a spirit prepared to follow them. Some censure them as too prodigal of their blood, and others commend their

[1] 'As the world grows old, it suffers illusions.'

courage and constancy; but where are they that sincerely resolve and prepare to be followers of them who through faith and patience inherit the promises? Heb. 6:12, or take them for an 'example of suffering, affliction, and of patience,' James 5:10.

It is as much our interest as it is our duty to be seasonably awakened out of our pleasant but most pernicious drowsiness. Troubles will be so much the more sinking and intolerable, by how much the more they steal upon us by way of surprizal. For look, as expectation deflowers any temporal comfort, by sucking out much of the sweetness thereof beforehand, and so we find the less in it when we come to the actual enjoyment: So the expectation of evils abates much of the dread and terror, by accustoming our thoughts beforehand to them, and making preparation for them: So that we find them not so grievous, amazing, and intolerable when they are come indeed.

This was exemplified to us very lively by holy Mr Bradford the martyr, when the keeper's wife came running into his chamber, saying, 'O Mr Bradford, I bring you heavy tidings, for tomorrow you must be burned, your chain is now buying, and presently you must go to Newgate.' He put off his hat, and looking up to heaven, said, 'O Lord, I thank thee for it; I have looked for this a long time; It comes not suddenly to me, the Lord make me worthy of it.' See in this example the singular advantage of a prepared and ready soul.

Reader, The cup of sufferings is a very bitter cup, and it is but needful that we provide somewhat to sweeten it, that we may be able to receive it with thanksgiving; and what those sweetening ingredients are, and how to prepare them, you will have some direction and help in the following discourse; which hath once already been presented to the public view; and that it may at this time also (wherein nothing can be more seasonable) become farther useful and assisting to the people of God in their present duties, is the hearty desire of

Thine and the Church's Servant in Christ,

JOHN FLAVEL.

Then Paul answered, What mean ye to weep, and to break my heart? For I am ready not to be bound only, but also to die at Jerusalem for the name of the Lord Jesus. – Acts 21:13.

Chapter 1

Wherein the text is opened, and the doctrine propounded.

THE Divine providence is not more signally discovered in governing the motions of the clouds, than it is in disposing and ordering the spirits and motions of the ministers of the gospel, who, in a mystical sense, are fruitful clouds, to dispense the showers of gospel blessings to the world. The motion of the clouds is not spontaneous, but they move as they are moved by the winds; neither can gospel ministers choose their own stations, and govern their own motions, but must go when and where the Spirit and providence of God directs and guides them; as will evidently appear in that dangerous voyage to Jerusalem in which the apostle was at this time engaged, Acts 20:22. 'And now, behold, I go bound in the Spirit to Jerusalem' [bound in the Spirit]: Alluding to the watery vapours which are bound up in clouds, and conveyed according to the motions of the wind. This journey was full of danger; Paul foresaw his business was not only to plant the gospel at Jerusalem with his doctrine, but to water it also with his blood; but so effectually was his will determined by the will of God, that he cheerfully complies with his duty therein, whatsoever difficulties and dangers did attend it.

And indeed it was his great advantage, that the will of God was so plainly and convincingly revealed to him touching this matter; for no sooner did he employ himself to obey this call of God, but he is presently assaulted by many strong temptations to decline it.

The first rub he met in his way was from the disciples of Tyre, who pretending to speak by the Spirit, said unto Paul, that he should not go up to Jerusalem, Acts 21:4. The Lord by this trying the spirit of his apostle much, as he did the young prophet coming from Judea to Bethel, 1 Kings 13:18, but not with like success.

His next discouragement was at Caesarea, where Agabus (whom Dorotheus affirms to be of the seventy-two disciples, and had before prophesied of the famine in the reign of Claudius, which accordingly came to pass) takes Paul's girdle, and binding his own hands and feet with it, said, 'Thus saith the Holy Ghost, so shall the Jews at Jerusalem bind the man that owneth this girdle, and shall deliver him into the hands of the Gentiles,' Acts 21:11. And surely he was not ignorant what he must expect whenever he should fall into their hands; yet neither could this affright him from his duty.

But then, last of all, he meeteth with the sorest trial from his dearest friends, who fell upon him with passionate entreaties and many tears, beseeching him to decline that journey: O they could not give up such a minister as Paul was! this even melted him down, and almost broke his heart, which yet was easier to do, than to turn him out of

[6]

the path of obedience: Where, by the way, we may note two things:

First, That divine precept, not providence, is to rule out our way of duty.

Secondly, That no hindrances or discouragements whatsoever will justify our neglect of a known duty.

All these rubs he passes over; all these discouragements he overcame, with this heroic and truly Christian resolution in the text; 'What mean ye to weep, and to break my heart? For I am ready not to be bound only, but also to die at Jerusalem, for the name of the Lord Jesus.'

In which words we have,

    1. A loving and gentle rebuke.
    2. A quieting and calming argument.

First, He lovingly and gently rebukes their fond and inordinate sorrow for his departure, in these words, *What mean ye to weep, and to break my heart?* As if he should say, What mean these passionate entreaties and tempting tears? To what purpose is all this ado? They are but so many snares of Satan, to turn my heart out of the way of obedience: You do as much as in you lies to break my heart; let there be no more of this I beseech you.

Secondly, He labours to charm their unruly passions with a very quieting and calming argument; For I am ready, etc. ἑτοίμως ἔχω [*hetoimos echo*], *parate habeo*. I am prepared and fitted for the greatest sufferings which shall befall me in the pursuit of my duty; be it a prison, or be it death, I am provided for either: Liberty is dear, and life much dearer, but Christ is dearer than either.

But what was there in all this, to satisfy them whose trouble it was to see him so forward? Let the words be considered, and we shall find divers things in them to satisfy and quiet their hearts, and make them willing to give him up.

First, I am ready; that is, God hath fitted and prepared my heart for the greatest sufferings; this is the work of God: flesh and blood would never be brought to this, were not all its interests and inclinations subdued, and overruled by the Spirit of God. What do ye therefore in all this, but work against the design of God, who hath fitted and prepared my heart for this service?

Secondly, I am ready; that is, my will and resolution stands in a full bent, my heart is fixed, you cannot therefore study to do me a greater injury, than to discompose and disorder my heart again, by casting such temptations as these in my way, to cause the flesh to rebel, and the enemy that is within to renew his opposition.

Thirdly, I am ready; that is, my heart is so fixed to follow the call of God, whatever shall befall me, that all your tears and entreaties to the contrary are but cast away; they cannot alter my fixed purpose; you had as good be quiet, and cheerfully resign me to the will of God.

Thus you see the equipage and preparation of Paul's spirit to receive both bonds and death for Christ at Jerusalem; this made him victorious over the temptations of friends, and the malice and cruelty of his enemies: By this readiness and preparation of his mind, he was carried through all, and enabled to finish his course with joy. From hence the observation is,

DOCTRINE. *That it is a blessed and excellent thing for the people of God to be prepared, and ready for the hardest services, and worst of sufferings, to which the Lord may call them.*

This is that which every gracious heart is reaching after, praying, and striving to obtain; but, ah! how few will attain it! Certainly there are not many among the multitudes of the professors of this generation that can say as Paul here did, 'I am ready to be bound, or to die for Christ.'

Chapter 2

Shews, that although God takes no delight in afflicting his people, yet he sometimes exposeth them to great and grievous sufferings; with a brief account why, and how he calls them thereunto.

THE mercies and compassions of God over his people are exceeding great and tender, Psalm 103:13, 'Like as a father pitieth his children, so the Lord pitieth them that fear him.' He delights not in afflicting and grieving them, Lam. 3:33, 'He doth not afflict willingly, nor grieve the children of men.' The scripture intimates to us a seeming conflict betwixt the justice and mercy of God, when he is about to deliver up his people into their enemies hands, Hosea 11:8, 9, 'How shall I give thee up, Ephraim? How shall I deliver thee, Israel? How shall I make thee as Admah? How shall I set thee as Zeboim? Mine heart is turned within me, my repentings are kindled together.' Which shews us with what reluctance and great unwillingness the Lord goes about such a work as this. The work of judgment is his *strange work*, it pleases him better to execute the milder attribute of mercy towards his children. Hence we find, when he is preparing to execute his judgments, that he delays the execution as long as the honour of his name and safety of his people will permit, Jer. 44:23. He bears till he can bear no longer: he often turns away his wrath from them, Psa. 78:38, 39. He tries them by lesser judgments and gentler corrections to prevent greater, Amos 4:6. When his people are humbled under the threatenings of his wrath, his heart is melted into compassion to them, Jer. 31:17, 20, and whenever his mercy prevails against judgment, it is with joy and triumph, James 2:13, *Mercy rejoiceth against judgment.*

For he feels his own tender compassions yearning over them; he foreseeth, and is no way willing to gratify the insulting pride of his and their enemies. Deut. 32:26, 27, 'I said, I would scatter them into corners, I would make the remembrance of them to cease from among men: were it not that I feared the wrath of the enemy, lest their adversaries should behave themselves strangely,' etc.

Yet all this, notwithstanding, it often falls out, by the provocations of his sons and daughters, that the Lord gives them up into the hands of their enemies for the correction of their evils, and the manifestation of his own glory. Seneca, though a heathen, could say, that God loves his people with a masculine love, not with a womanish indulgence and tenderness: If need require, they shall be in heaviness through manifold temptations, 1 Pet. 1:6. He had rather their hearts should be heavy under adversity, than vain and careless under prosperity; the choicest spirits have been exercised with the sharpest sufferings, and those that now shine as stars in heaven, have been trod underfoot as dung on the earth. 1 Cor. 4:11-13, 'Unto this present hour we both hunger, and thirst, and are naked, and buffeted, and have no certain dwelling-place; and labour working with our hands: being reviled, we bless; being persecuted, we suffer it: being defamed we intreat: we are made as the filth of the world, and the offscouring of all things unto this day.' The eleventh chapter to the Hebrews is a compendium of the various and grievous sufferings of the primitive saints: 'They were tortured, they were sawn asunder, were tempted, were slain with the sword, they wandered about in sheepskins and goatskins, being afflicted, destitute, tormented, of whom the world was not worthy, they wandered in deserts, and in mountains, in dens, and in caves of the earth.' And since the earth hath dried up those rivers of precious blood, whereof the sacred records make mention, what seas of Christians' blood have since those days been shed by bloody persecutors? Histories inform us that in the ten primitive persecutions, so many of the saints and martyrs of Jesus Christ have been slain, as that you may allow five thousand a day to every day in the whole year. Those bloody emperors sported themselves with the death of God's dearest saints; many precious Christians were burnt by night at Rome, to serve as torches to light their enemies in the passage through the streets; eight hundred thousand martyrs are mentioned within the space of thirty years, since the Jesuits arose out of the bottomless pit.

To what grievous sufferings did the Lord give up those precious servants of Christ, the Waldenses and Albigenses, who received the light of reformation about the year 1260, when the fogs of Antichristian darkness overspread the earth! a people sound in judgment, as appears by their letters, catechisms, and confessions, which are extant; a people of a simple, plain, and inoffensive behaviour: Yet, with what fury and rage did that impious pope Pius persecute them to destruction! driving them into the woods and mountains, except the aged, and children that could not flee, who were murdered in the way: Some famished in the caves and clefts of the rocks; others endured the rack for eight hours together; some beaten with iron rods, others thrown from the tops of high towers, and dashed to pieces.

What bloody shambles and slaughter-houses have France, Ireland, and England, been made by popish cruelty! More might be related out of each story than a tender hearted reader is able to bear the rehearsal of. But what God hath done, he may do again: We are not better than our fathers, dismal clouds of indignation are gathering over our heads, charged with double destruction; should the Lord please to make them break upon us; we cannot imagine the rage of Satan to be abated, now that his kingdom hastens to its period, Rev. 12:12, nor are his instruments grown less cruel and skilful to destroy. The land, indeed, hath enjoyed a long rest, and this generation is acquainted with little more of martyrdom, than what the histories of former times inform us of: But yet let no man befool himself with a groundless expectation of continuing tranquillity. Augustine thinks that the bloody sweat which overran the body of Christ in the garden, signified the sharp and grievous sufferings which in his mystical body he should afterwards endure; and indeed it is a truth, that these are also called the remains of Christ's sufferings, Col. 1:24. His *personal sufferings* were indeed completed at his resurrection, that cup was full to the brim, to which no drop of sufferings can be added; but his sufferings in his mystical body are not yet full; by his personal sufferings he fully satisfied the wrath of God, but the sufferings of his people have not yet satisfied the wrath of men: Though millions of precious saints have shed their blood for Christ, whose souls are now crying under the altar, *How long, Lord! how long!* yet there are many more coming on behind in the same path of persecution, and much Christian blood must yet be shed, before the mystery of God be finished; and notwithstanding this lucid interval, the clouds seem to be returning again after the rain. Thus you see to what grievous sufferings the merciful God hath sometimes called his dearest people.

Now God may be said to call forth his people to suffer, when he so hedgeth them in by providence, that there is no way to escape suffering, but by sinning; whatsoever providence labours with such a dilemma as this, is a plain signification of God's will to us in that case. We may not now expect extraordinary calls to suffering work, as some of the saints had of old, Gen. 22:2, Acts 9:16, but when our way is so shut up by providence, that we cannot avoid suffering, but by stepping over the hedge of the command, God will have us look upon that exigence as his call to suffer: And if the reasons be demanded, why the Lord, who is inclined to mercy, doth often hedge in his own people, by his providence, in a suffering path; let us know, that in so doing, he doth both,

1. Illustrate his own glory. And,
2. Promote his people's happiness.

First, Hereby the most wise God doth illustrate the glory of his own name, clearing up the righteousness of his ways by the sufferings of his own people: By this the word shall see, that how well soever he loves them, he will not indulge or patronize their sins; if they will be so disingenuous to abuse his favours, he will be so just to make them suffer for their sins, and by those very sufferings will provide for his own glory, which was by them clouded in the eyes of the world. He hates not sin a jot the less, because it is found in his own people, Amos 3:2. And though, for the magnifying of his mercy, he will pardon their sins, yet for the clearing of his righteousness, he will take vengeance upon their inventions, Psa. 99:8.

Moreover, by exposing his people to such grievous sufferings, he gives a fit opportunity to manifest the glory of his power in their support, and of his wisdom, in the marvellous ways of their escape and deliverance. It is one of the greatest wonders in the world, how the church subsists under such fierce and frequent assaults as are made upon it by enemies. 'I will turn aside (said Moses), and see this great sight, why the bush is not consumed,' Exod. 3:3. That flaming bush was a lively emblem of the oppressed church in Egypt; the crackling flames noted the heat of their persecution, the remaining of the bush unconsumed in the flames, signified the wonderful power of God in their preservation: No people are so privileged, so protected, so delivered, as the people of God. Much less opposition than hath been made against the church, have overturned, and utterly destroyed, the mighty monarchies of the world.

> —*Sic Medus ademit*
> *Assyrio, Medoque tulit moderamina Perses,*
> *Subjecit Persen Macedo, cessurus et ipse*
> *Romanis—*[1]

> Assyria's empire thus the Mede did shake,
> The Persian next, the pride of Media brake;
> Then Persia sunk by Macedonia prest,
> That, in its turn, fell by Rome at last.—

---

[1] Claudian, lib. 3. *in laudes Stillicones.*

And no less admirable is the wisdom of God, in frustrating and defeating the most deep and desperate designs of hell, against his poor people. Now, you may see the most wise God going beyond a malicious and subtle devil, overturning in a moment the deep laid designs and contrivances of many years, and that at the very birth and point of execution, Esth. 7:10, snaring the wicked in the works of their own hands; making their own tongues to fall upon them; working out such marvellous salvations with his own hand, as fills them with astonishment and wonder, Psa. 126:1, 'When the Lord turned back the captivity of Zion, we were like them that dreamed.'

Secondly, As God provides for his own glory, by the sufferings and troubles of his people; so he advanceth their happiness, and greatly promotes their interest thereby.

For, *First*, These troubles are ordered as so many occasions and means to mortify the corruptions that are in their hearts; there are rank weeds springing up in the best soil, which need such winter weather to rot them: And, certainly, if we reckon humility, heavenly mindedness, contempt of the world, and longing desires after heaven, to be the real interest and advantage of the church; then it is evident, nothing so much promotes their interest, as a suffering condition doth: Adversity kills those corruptions which prosperity bred.

Secondly, By these trials their sincerity is cleared, to the joy and satisfaction of their own hearts; many a doubt and fear, which had long entangled and perplexed them, is removed and answered. When adversity hath given them proof, and trial of their own hearts, one sharp trial wherein

God helps us to be faithful, will do more to satisfy our fears, and resolve our doubts, than all the sermons that ever we heard in our lives could do.

Thirdly, These sufferings and trials of the church, are ordained to free it of abundance of hypocrites, which were its reproach, as well as burden, Amos 9:9, 10. Affliction is a furnace to separate the dross from the more pure and noble gold. Multitudes of hypocrites like flies in a hot summer, are generated by the church's prosperity; but this winter weather kills them: Many gaudy professors grow within the enclosure of the church, like beautiful flowers in the field, where they stand during its peace and prosperity, in the pride and bravery of their gifts and professions; but the wind passeth over them, and they are gone, and their places shall know them no more; to allude to that in Psalm 103:16. Thunder and lightning is very terrible weather, but exceeding useful to purify and cleanse the air.

Fourthly, The church's sufferings are ordered and sanctified, to endear them to each other. Times of common suffering, are times of reconciliation, and greater endearments among the people of God; never more endeared, than when most persecuted; never more united, than when most scattered, Mal. 3:16, 'Then they that feared the Lord, spake often one to another.' Certainly there is something in our fellowship in the same sufferings, that is endearing and engaging; but there is much more in the discoveries that persecution makes of the sincerity of our hearts, which, it may be, was before entertained with jealousy; and there is yet more than all this in the reproofs of the rod, whereby they are humbled for their pride, wantonness, and bitterness of their spirits to each other, and made to cry, in the sense of these transgressions, as Psa. 79:8, 'Remember not against us former iniquities.'

Lastly, By these troubles and distresses, they are awakened to their duties, and taught to pray more frequently, spiritually, and fervently. Ah! what drowsiness and formality is apt to creep in upon the best hearts, in the time of prosperity; but when the storm rises, and the sea grows turbulent and raging, now they cry as the disciples to Christ, *Lord, save us, we perish*. They say music is sweetest upon the waters; I am sure the sweetest melody of prayer is upon the deep waters of affliction: For these, among many other righteous, wise, and holy ends, the Lord permits and orders the persecutions and distresses of his people.

Chapter 3

Shews that it is usual with God to premonish his people of approaching trials and sufferings; with some account of the manner how, and the reason why he so forewarns them.

As Paul had many clear premonitions and fore-notices of the sufferings that should befall him at Jerusalem, that he might not be surprised by them when they came; so it is usual with God (though not in such an immediate and extraordinary a manner) to admonish the world, and especially his own people, of great trials and sufferings beforehand. Amos 3:7, 'Surely the Lord will do nothing, but he revealeth his secrets unto his servants the prophets.'

Thus, when he was about to bring the flood upon the world, he gave one hundred and twenty years warning of it before it came, Gen. 6:3, and when he was to destroy Sodom, he saith, Gen. 18:17, 'Shall I hide from Abraham the thing that I do?' And the like discovery he made about the same judgment to Lot, Gen. 19:12-14. So when the captivity of the Jews was nigh at hand, the people had many forewarnings of it; God forewarned them both *ministerially* and *providentially*; i.e. warned them by the prophets, Ezek. 3:17, 'Hear the word of my mouth, and give them warning from me.' And when the time drew nigh to execute the judgment determined upon Jerusalem, and the temple, how plainly did Christ foretell them of it? Luke 19:43, 44, 'Thine enemies shall cast a trench about thee, and compass thee round, and keep thee in on every side, and shall lay thee even with the ground, and thy children within thee.'

And when the storm was just ready to fall,[1] their own historian tells us, a voice was heard in the temple, saying, *Migremus hinc*, Let us go hence. 'Which voice[2] Tacitus also mentions in his annals, affirming it to be more than a human voice, telling them God was departing, and that it was accompanied with a rushing noise, as of persons going out. These were extraordinary warnings.' The like signs have been given to divers other nations, by dreadful *eclipses* of the heavenly bodies, *portentous comets, earthquakes*, and other signs of judgment.

Now, though we have no ground to expect such extraordinary warnings, yet we have the most apparent and certain signs of approaching calamities; after which, if they surprize us, the fault must lie in our own inexcusable negligence; for we have a standing rule to govern ourselves in this matter, and that is this; 'When the same sins are found in one nation, which have brought down the wrath of God upon another nation, it is an evident sign of judgment at the door; for God is unchangeable, just, and holy, and will not favour that in one people which he hath punished in another, nor bless that in one age which he hath cursed

---

[1] Josephus *de bello Jud.* lib. 7, cap. 2.

[2] *Audita major humana vox excedere Deos, simul ingens motus excedentium*, Tacitus, *Histories* 5:13:3. 'A voice more powerful than from any human being was heard saying that the gods were departing, and at the same time a great movement among the departing gods could be heard.'

in another.' Upon this very ground it was that the apostle warned the Corinthians, by the example of the Israelites, whose sins had ruined them in the wilderness, 1 Cor. 10:6, 'Now these things were our examples, to the intent we should not lust after evil things, as they also lusted.' As if he should say, Look upon those dead bodies which are, as it were, cast up upon the scripture-shore for a warning to you: Follow not the same course, lest you meet in the same curse; if you tread the same paths, expect the same punishment. God is as righteous now as he was then: he hates, and will punish sin in you as much as he did in them.

Let us therefore consider what those provocations were, that hastened the wrath of God upon his own Israel, a people that were nigh and dear unto him: a people upon whom he spent as much of the riches of his patience, as upon any people in the world; that so we may reckon whereabout we are at this day, and what is like to be the lot of this sinful and provoking generation; and we shall find, by the consent of all the prophets, that these sins were the immediate forerunners, and proper causes of their overthrow.

First, The great corruption of God's worship among them kindled his wrath, and hastened their ruin, Psa. 106:39-42. 'They were defiled with their own works, and went a whoring with their own inventions; therefore was the wrath of God kindled against his people, insomuch that he abhorred his own inheritance, and he gave them into the hand of the heathen; and they that hated them ruled over them; their enemies also oppressed them, and they were brought into subjection under their hand.' They that will not bear the golden yoke of Christ, shall be galled with

[23]

the iron yoke of men: nothing more provokes the anger of God than the adulterating of his worship; a man will bear a thousand infirmities in the wife of his bosom, but unfaithfulness in the marriage-covenant breaks his heart. After the manner of men, so abused and grieved, the Lord expresseth himself, Ezek. 6:9, 'I am broken with their whorish heart, which have departed from me, and with their eyes, that go a whoring after their idols.' Men cannot invent a surer and speedier way to their own ruin, than to bring their own inventions into God's worship.

Secondly, Incorrigible obstinacy and impenitency, under gentler strokes and lesser judgments, make way for utter ruin and desolation, Amos 4 from the 6th to the 12th verse. Scarcity, mildews, pestilence, and sword, had been tried upon them, but without effect; for the remnant that escaped those judgments (although plucked as so many brands out of the fire, in which their fellow sinners perished) were not reformed by those gentler and *moderated* judgments.

Thirdly, Stupidity and senselessness of God's hand, and the tokens of his anger, were provoking causes and forerunners of their national desolation; they neither saw the hand of God when it was lifted up, nor humbled themselves under it when it was laid on; the hand of God is then said to be *lifted up*, when the providences of God prepare and posture themselves for our affliction. When the clouds of judgment gather over our heads, and grow blacker and blacker, as theirs did upon them, and do upon us at this day, but they took no notice of it, Isa. 26:11, 'Lord, when thy hand is lifted up, they will not see'; and (which is the height of stupidity) they all remained senseless and regardless, when the hand of God was laid upon them, Isa. 42:24, 25, 'Who gave Jacob for a spoil, and Israel to the robbers? Did not the Lord, he against whom we have sinned? for they would not walk in his ways, neither were they obedient to his law. Therefore he hath poured upon them the fury of his anger, and the strength of battle: and it hath set him on fire round about, yet he knew not; and it burned him, yet he laid it not to heart.'

O prodigious sottishness! It was not some small drops of God's anger, but *the fury of his anger*; not some lighter skirmish of his judgments with them, but *the strength of battle*: It was not some particular stroke upon single persons or families, but *it set him on fire round about*, a general conflagration; yet all this would not awaken them.

Fourthly, The persecution of God's faithful ministers and people were another sin that procured, and a sign that foretold the destruction of their nation, 2 Chron. 36:15, 16, 'And the Lord God of their fathers sent to them by his messengers, rising up betimes, and sending; because he had compassion on his people, and on his dwelling-place: but they mocked the messengers of God, and despised his words, and misused his prophets, until the wrath of the Lord arose against his people, till there was no remedy.' There were also a number of upright souls among them, who desired to worship God according to his own prescription; but a snare was laid for them in Mizpah, and a net spread for them upon Tabor, Hos. 5:1, and this hastened judgment towards them: Mizpah and Tabor were places lying in the way betwixt Samaria and Jerusalem, where the true worship of God was: and in those places spies were set by the priests to observe and inform against them; so that

[25]

it became very hazardous to attend the pure and incorrupt worship of God, which quickly hastened on their ruin.

Fifthly, The removal of godly and useful men by death, in more than ordinary haste, was to them a sign of desolation at hand. Isa. 57:1, 'The righteous perisheth, and no man layeth it to heart'; and merciful men are taken away, none considering that the righteous is taken away from the evil to come.' In this case God acts towards his people, as the husbandman in a catching harvest doth by his corn; he hurries it with a shuffling haste into the barn when he sees a storm coming: or as a careful father with his sons that are abroad at school, who sends his horses to fetch them home speedily, when he hears the plague is begun in the place. Upon this ground the prophet Micah bewails himself, Micah 7:1, 'Woe is me! for I am as when they have gathered the summerfruits, as the grape gleanings of the vintage: there is no cluster to eat: my soul desired the firstripe fruit.' Q. d.[1] Alas! Alas! what miserable days are at hand! what miseries must I expect to see! The pleasant clusters, i.e. the societies of the saints are gathered away by the hand of death; there are but few that remain, here and there a single saint, like grapes after the vintage is done, two or three upon the utmost branches.

Sixthly, The general decay of the life and power of godliness among them that were loft, foreboded destruction at the door: this is both a provoking sin, and a fore-running sign of national calamity. Hos. 4:18, *Their drink is sour.* A metaphor lively expressing the deadness and formality of

---

[1] Q. d. = *Quasi Dicat* (Latin: as if he would say).

the people in the worship of God. It was like sour or dead drink, which hath lost its spirit and relish, and is become flat. Such were their duties; no spiritual life, affection, or savour in them: they heard as if they heard not, and prayed as if they prayed not; the ordinances of God were to them as the ordinances of men, of which the apostle saith, that they perish in the using.

Seventhly, To conclude; Mutual animosities, jars, and divisions, were to them manifest symptoms of national calamities and desolations: for then Ephraim envied Judah, and Judah vexed Ephraim, Isa. 11:13; Hos. 9:7, 'The days of visitation are come, the days of recompence are come; Israel shall know it: the prophet is a fool, the spiritual man is mad, for the multitude of thine iniquity, and the great hatred.'

When such symptoms of God's indignation do appear upon any people, the Lord, by them, as by so many glaring meteors and blazing comets, forewarns the world that his judgments are near, even at the door. These signs all men ought to observe, and behold with trembling. If you ask, why doth God usually give such warnings of his indignation before it comes? The reasons are,

1. To prevent the execution.
2. To make them more tolerable.
3. To leave the incorrigible inexcusable.

First, Warning is given, with design to prevent the execution of judgments, Amos 4:12, 'Therefore thus will I do unto thee, O Israel: and because I will do this unto thee, prepare to meet thy God, O Israel'; i.e. Prepare thyself to meet me in the way of my judgments, by humiliation and intercession to prevent the execution. And what else was the design of God in sending Jonah to the great city Nineveh, but to excite them to repentance for the prevention of their ruin. This Jonah knew to be the Lord's meaning, how positive soever the words of his commission were; and therefore he declined the message to secure his credit; knowing, that if upon warning given they repented, the gracious nature of God would soon melt into compassion over them, and free grace would make him appear as a liar; for so we must expound his words, Jonah 4:2, 'Was not this my saying, when I was yet in my country? Therefore I fled before unto Tarshish: for I knew that thou art a gracious God, and merciful, slow to anger, and of great kindness, and repentest thee of the evil.' Q. d. Yea, Lord, I knew beforehand it would come to this; thou sendest me positively to denounce thy judgments to Nineveh, meantime desiring nothing more than the execution of them might be prevented by their repentance. And thus thy mercy hath exposed my reputation, in saving them from destruction.

Secondly, God forewarns his people of judgments, to make them more tolerable when they come; expected evils are nothing so heavy as those that come by surprisal; for look, as the expectation of a mercy makes it less sweet, our thoughts having anticipated and sucked out much of the sweetness beforehand; so the expectation of judgments before they befall us, make them less bitter and burdensome than else they would be, the soul having inured and accustomed itself to them, by frequent thoughts, and prepared and made ready itself to entertain them, as Paul did in my text. To prevent the disciples surprisal and offence at those days of persecution that were coming upon them, Christ foretold them, and gave them fair warning before-hand, John 16:4.

Thirdly, He forewarns his people of approaching dangers, to leave the incorrigible wholly inexcusable, that those who have no sense of sin, nor care to prevent ruin, might have no cloak for their folly when judgments overtake them, 'What wilt thou say when he shall punish thee?' Jer. 13:21, 22. As if he should say, What plea, or apology is loft thee, after so many fair warnings and timely premonitions? Thou canst not say, I have surprised thee, or that thou wast ruined before thou wast warned. Thy destruction therefore is of thyself.

Chapter 4

Demonstrating the excellency of a prepared heart for the worst of sufferings; and what a blessed thing it is to be ready to be bound, or to die for Christ, as Paul here was.

[I *AM ready.*] O blessed frame of spirit! how hard, but how happy is it to get a heart so tempered! Every Christian can say, I would be ready, and the Lord make me ready for sufferings; but few can say, I am ready, my heart is prepared and fitted for such a work: yet this example shews us it is attainable: and what a blessed thing it is to attain it, the following particulars will abundantly convince us.

First, Readiness for sufferings will bring the heart of a Christian to an holy rest and tranquillity, in a suffering hour, and prevent that anxiety, perturbation, and distraction of mind, which puts the sinking weight into afflictions. The more cares, fears, and troubles we have before our sufferings come, the more calm, quiet, and composed we are like to be when our sufferings are come indeed. It is admirable to consider with what peace and patience Job entertained his troubles, which, considering the kinds, degrees, and manner in which they befell him, one would think they should at least have startled and amazed him, and put his soul (as gracious and mortified as it was) into great disorder and confusion; but you find the contrary:

never did the patience of a man triumph at that rate over adversity; he worships God, owns his hand, and resigns himself up to his pleasure, Job 1:20, 21. And whence was this? Surely had his troubles come by way of surprise, he could never have carried it at that rate; but in the days of his peace and prosperity he had prepared for such a day as this, Job 3:25, 26, 'I was not in safety, neither had I rest; yet trouble came; the thing that I feared (saith he) is come upon me.' He laid it to heart before it came, and therefore it neither distracted, nor brake the heart when it came. In like manner the prophet Habakkuk stood upon his watch-tower, i.e. he made his observations by the word upon the probable events of providence, whereby he got a clear fore-sight of those troublesome days that were at hand; which though it made him tremble in himself, yet it gave him rest in the day of evil, Hab. 3:16-18. There is a twofold rest in the day of evil, viz.

1. A rest of deliverance.
2. A rest of contentation.

It is a singular mercy to find rest in a man's own spirit; to enjoy inward peace, and tranquillity of mind, when there is no rest without; and the way to obtain this, is to fore-see, count upon, and make due preparation for troublous times beforehand: evils that come by way of surprisal, are not only amazing, but very frequently destructive evils; it is a sad aggravation to feel a misery, before we fear it; those calamities that find men secure, do usually leave them *desperate*; the enemy that comes upon our backs hath a great advantage to ruin us, yet this is the common case of the world, 'For man knoweth not his time, but as the fishes are taken in an evil net, and as the birds that are caught in the snare; so are the sons of men snared in an evil time, when it falleth on them suddenly,' Eccles. 9:12. Thus perished the old world; there was but one Noah provided for the flood, and he only, with his family, was preserved in it: all the rest were eating, drinking, marrying, and giving in marriage, until the flood came and swept them all away, Matt. 24:38. Men will not use their foreseeing faculties; but because it is all quiet today, they conclude it shall be so tomorrow. Those that are at rest in their habitation, and have got a safe pillow under their heads, are apt to fall asleep in security, and dream pleasantly of continued rest and peace; and loath they are to interrupt their sensual pleasure with melancholy thoughts of changes and sufferings.

Philosophers tell us, that immediately before an earthquake the air is very quiet and serene; and before the great rain falls, the wind is usually still: were the aspect of second causes much more favourable and encouraging than it is; yet there is cause enough, for all that are wise in heart, to fear and tremble, under the consideration of that national guilt which is treasured up, and will certainly produce distress and trouble.

O Christians! look out for days of visitation; prepare for a storm, and provide you an ark, an hiding-place in Christ, and the promises, as ever you expect rest, and peace in your own spirits, when the earth shall be full of tumults, uproars, and desolations.

Secondly, Our preparation for sufferings is an excellent argument of the honesty and sincerity of our hearts, in the matters of religion: he that makes account of sufferings, and is daily at work with his own heart, mortifying his corruptions, weaning its worldly affections, exciting and making ready its suffering-graces, resolving in the strength of God, to take his lot with Christ, wherever, and howsoever it shall fall; this is the man that hath deliberately closed with Christ upon his own terms, and is like to be the durable and victorious Christian.

As for hypocrites (Christ's summer friends), they have either their exceptions against the severities of religion, and study to secure to themselves a retreat from danger, or else they rush inconsiderately into the profession of Christ, never debating the terms which he proposes to all that will follow him, Mark 8:34. The necessity of a rational and well-advised closure with Christ upon suffering and self-denying terms, is by himself fully set forth in that excellent parable, Luke 14:25-28. There was a great multitude that followed him at that time; Christ began to grow in request among them; they flocked from all parts to see and hear him; but he foresaw, that if once a sharp trial should befall them, it would quickly thin, and diminish that great multitude, and reduce them like Gideon's host, into a little handful: and therefore he resolves to deal candidly and plainly with them; he propounds his terms, and sets down his conditions, which every one of them must subscribe, that will follow him; the sum of which is this, 'Let him deny himself, take up his cross and follow me.' And to evince the rationality of these terms, he argues, from the most common and obvious practices of men in their civil affairs: no man, that exerciseth reason, will begin to build an house, and lay a large foundation, when he is not provided with a stock to carry up the walls, and complete the work: no man, in his wits would engage with a handful of men, against a great and armed multitude; possibly they may intend to *face*, but no man would think they intend to *fight* the enemy, on such a disadvantage. Just so stands the case in our profession of Christ; if we really intend to go through with the business of religion, we must sit down, and compute the cost and charges of Christianity, think upon the worst, as well as the best, reckon upon reproaches, prisons, and death for his sake, as well as the easier and more pleasant parts of active obedience; and having so done, if then we can be content to run all hazards, and forego all the rest upon his account, and accordingly manage ourselves in a day of suffering, then we deal with Christ, and clear ourselves from the danger of hypocrisy. It is for want of this, that so many professors faint, and fall away, in times of temptation, furnishing the devil with so many triumphs over religion, and the more upright professors of it. It was for want of *depth of earth*, (i.e.) a deep consideration, and well-rooted resolution at first, that the stony-ground hypocrite so quickly withered away, when the sun of persecution began to shine fervently upon him, Matt. 13:5, 6. And doubtless it is to prevent this fatal issue of our profession, that God makes such deep wounds by conviction upon his people's hearts at first; it is for our establishment in future trials, and sufferings, that he so distresses, and humbles them; that he makes sin so bitter and burdensome to them; as well knowing that all this is no more than needs, to prevent their returning again to sin, in the times of their temptation.

O professor! if thou be one that art come to Christ in this way, and hast thus deliberately closed with him; if thou hast as well bethought thyself of bearing his cross, as of wearing his crown; thou hast then a fair evidence of the uprightness of thy heart, than which, the world affords not a sweeter comfort.

Thirdly, The advantage of preparation for suffering lies in this, that it prevents, and cuts off the scandal and offence of the cross, with respect both to ourselves and others.

First, It prevents our own offence at sufferings; and by Christ's own testimony, that soul is blessed, that is not offended in him, Matt. 11:6. Among the multitudes of professors, few are found that are no way offended at suffering for Christ; they expected much peace, honour, and prosperity in the ways of religion, but finding their expectations frustrated, and their carnal interest rather exposed, than secured by their profession of Christ, they go back like those in John 6:66 and walk no more with him. And it is very remarkable, that Christ dates the offence that men shall take at him, from the first appearance of suffering, Matt. 24:8, 10, 'All these are the beginnings of sorrows, and then shall many be offended.' Sorrows and apostasies commence together.

But, reader, if thou be one that makest it thy business to foresee, and prepare for an evil day, thou wilt have as good thoughts of Christ, and his ways at the lowest ebb, as ever thou hadst in the greatest flourish, and time of prosperity. 'Great peace (saith the Psalmist) have they that love thy law, and nothing shall offend them.' O happy soul! whom no troubles, reproaches or sufferings, are able to offend! thou mayest meet with prisons, death, banishments, yea, but none of these things shall offend, or stumble thee, but thou shalt peaceably and safely pass over them, because they are no more than thou expectedst, and providest for.

Secondly, And by this means thou wilt also prevent the offence and scandals of *others* at the ways of religion. It is a sad, and dangerous thing to be an occasion of stumbling, either to the weak or to the wicked. 'Woe to the world because of offences, for it must needs be that offences come; but woe to that man by whom the offence cometh,' Matt. 18:7. The apostasies and sinful compliances of ungrounded professors and weak Christians in times of temptation, are the woeful occasions of prejudicing others against religion, and shedding the blood of souls. Ah! it were much better never to be in the ways of profession, than to be there only as a stone of stumbling, and a rock of offence to others: but all this mischief will be prevented by thy serious expectation of, and provision for the evil day.

Fourthly, A fourth excellency of preparation for sufferings lies in this, that it hath a tendency to convince and awaken the drowsy world. O! if the Lord's people would but engage in this work in earnest, and live as people that are providing for a storm, and resolve, in the strength of God, to run all hazards and hardships for Christ, I am persuaded it would be of more use to startle, and convince the world, than all the sermons that ever they heard: for here is that which dashes and cuts the throat of all our labours. We preach up self-denial, and contempt of life, and liberty for Christ: now though they hear us preach the necessity, and excellency of these things, and hear you profess them as your principles; yet when they look upon the lives of professors in times of danger, and find no proportion betwixt profession and practice; when they see us cling to the world, and are as loath to give it up as others; when they observe prisons and sufferings affright and terrify us as much as those that make no profession; when they see us start like hares, at every sound, and that we live not loose from the world, as men prepared to let it go and give it up for Christ: why then they conclude that we dare not trust our own principles, when it comes to the push. And how can they be persuaded to believe that which they think we ourselves do not really believe, although we persuade them to believe it?

My friends, the world hath *eyes* to see what you can *do*, as well as *ears* to hear what you can *say*; and as long as they see you do no more than others, you may talk your hearts out ere they will believe your way is better than others.

But now when persecution ariseth, did they see you providing yourselves for it, and putting on your harness to enter the lists, carry your dearest enjoyments in your hands, and put on the shoe of preparation, to follow the Lord through the roughest ways of sufferings; this would convince to purpose, and preach the excellency of Christ, the vanity of the creature, the rationality and certainty of Christian principles, in a more intelligible and rousing dialect to them, than all our cheap and easy commendations of them did. And hence it is that Noah was said to condemn the world, Heb. 11:7, 'By faith Noah, being warned of God of things not seen as yet,' i.e. of the deluge that was coming, though no appearance of it yet, the heavens being as clear as ever; yet believing the threatening, 'He was moved with fear.' The fear of God, an effect of his faith in the word of God, *moved* (i.e.) impelled him to his duty; set him about his preparation work to provide an *ark*, and this was it by which he *condemned the world*, left them excuseless. For they not only heard of an approaching flood by his minis-try, but now saw he himself believed what he preached, by his daily preparations against it came. O consider this, how much it would tend to the world's conviction; now they will see that you are in good earnest, and that there is a reality in godliness: this will induce them to search into the matter more than ever, and remove those prejudices they have taken up against the good ways of God, as if they were but *phantasms* and conceits.

Fifthly, In the next place, this foresight and preparation must needs be an excellent thing, because the Spirit of God everywhere sets an honourable character upon it, and always mentions such persons with some singular com-mendation and respect. These only were wise men in the judgment of God, and all the rest (what great politicians soever they are famed to be among men) are accounted fools, Prov. 22:3; Eccles. 2:14. 'The wise man's eyes are in his head'; that is, he is a fore-seeing man; 'but the fool goes on, and is punished': Rushes on without consideration, sus-pecting no danger that he at present sees not, and so smarts for his folly. Beloved, there are *signs of the times*, as well as of the weather, Matt. 16:3. You may see the clouds of judg-ment gathering before the storm falls upon you. And this is the meaning of Zeph. 2:1, 2, 'Gather yourselves together, before the decree bring forth, and the day pass as the chaff': where there is a *conception* of judgment there will be a *birth*, unless the reformations and prayers of the saints cause it to miscarry. But it requires wisdom to discern this; they must be men of much observation that can descry it at a great distance; yet this may be done by considering what God hath done in like cases in former ages, when nations have been guilty of the same sins as now they are: For God is as just now as then, and hates sin as much as ever he did; and partly by attending to things *present*, to what fulness and maturity the sins of a nation are grown, Joel 3:16, or what beginnings of judgment are already upon a people, as harbingers and forerunners of more at hand, Luke 23:30, 31, 1 Sam. 2:12. Or what is the universal note and cry of God's ministers, who are his watchmen to foresee danger, Ezek. 3:17, and his trumpeters to discover it, Num. 10:8. And when these have one mouth given them, certainly there is much in it, Luke 1:70. Or, lastly, by pondering those scripture-prophecies that yet remain to be fulfilled. They must all go out their times, and accomplish their full number of years and months; but certainly they shall be fulfilled in their seasons.

By attending to these things, a Christian may give a near guess at the judgments that are approaching a nation, and so order himself accordingly. Eccles. 8:5, 'A wise man's heart discerns both time and judgment.' And this is (even in the judgment of God) a choice point of wisdom; whereas, on the contrary, heedless and careless ones, that regard not these things are branded for fools, and upbraided with more brutishness than the beasts of the field, or fowls of the air, Matt. 16:3; Jer. 8:7, 'The stork in the heavens, the swallow, turtle, and crane,' observe their seasons of departing, and returning upon the approach of the *winter* and *spring*, and that by a natural instinct, whereby they prolong their lives, which else must perish. But though God hath made man wiser than the fowls of the air, and beasts of the earth, which by instinct will quit colder climates, or run to the hedges when winter, or storms approach; yet the heavens may be astonished at this, to see nature cast by sin so far below itself; and that in reasonable creatures.

But now, if this be foreseen, then there is a singular advantage in a man's hand, either to use the means of preventing those approaching calamities, Zeph. 2:3. or if it cannot be prevented, yet to take sanctuary in Christ, Mic. 5:5, to run to the promises and attributes, Isa. 26:20, 21, and so have a good roof over his head while the storm falls and the weather is tempestuous abroad. And therefore certainly this preparation is an excellent thing. Whatever the Spirit of God speaks in the commendation of foreseeing evils, is with respect to this duty of preparing for them; for foresights of evils without preparation, rather increases than diminishes the misery.

A *sixth* excellency of preparation lies in the influence that it hath into a Christian's stability in the evil day. You cannot but know that your stability in that critical hour of temptation, is a choice and singular mercy, inasmuch as all you are worth in the other world depends upon your standing then, Rev. 21:7, 8, Rom. 2:6, 7, Luke 22:27, neither can you be ignorant how much you are like to be tried, and put to it then, whether you respect the enemy that engages you, Eph. 6:12, or your own weakness, who have been so often foiled in lesser trials, Jer. 12:5. All the grace you have will be little enough to keep the field and bear you up from sinking; and therefore it cannot but be a blessed thing, to be able to stand and cope with the greatest difficulties in such a time of trial as that will be. 'Now he that expects to do this must put on the whole armour of God.' See Eph. 6:12-14. There is no expectation of standing in the evil day, except *your foot be shod*, that is, your wills prepared with the *preparation of the gospel of peace.*

It is true, that our ability to stand is not from our own inherent grace; 'For by his strength shall no man prevail,' 1 Sam. 2:9. And yet it is as true, that without grace, both inherent in us, and excited and prepared for a storm, we cannot expect to stand; For these two, grace inherent in us, and grace exciting and assisting without are not *opposed*, but *co-ordinated*. Grace in us, is the weapon by which our enemy falls: but then that weapon must be managed by the hand of the Spirit. – Well then, look upon this as a choice mercy, which tends so much to your stability.

A *seventh* excellency of a prepared heart, is that it is a very high testification of our love to Jesus Christ, when we thus shew our willingness to take our lot with him, and follow him wherever he goes. What an high expression of love was that of Ruth to her mother Naomi? 'I will not go back, but where thou lodgest I will lodge, and where thou goest I will go.' It is excellent when a soul can say to Christ, as Ittai to David, 2 Sam. 15:21, 'Surely in what place my lord the king shall be, whether in death or in life, even there also will thy servant be.' This is love indeed, to cleave to him in a time of such distresses and dangers. This is 'love which the waters cannot quench, nor the floods drown,' Song of Sol. 8:7. *Probatio amoris, est exhibitio operis*: If you love Christ indeed, shew your love by some fruits of it; and surely this is a very choice fruit, and proof of it. There are many that profess a great deal of love to Christ, but when it comes to this touch-stone, it appears false and counterfeit; but a mere flourish when no danger is near. But that soul which buckles on the shoe of preparation, to follow him through thorns and briers, and over the rocks and mountains of difficulties and troubles, loves him indeed, Jer. 2:2, 3. Beloved, it is one of the choicest discoveries of your love to your master Christ, yea, it is such a testification of love to him, as angels are not capable of. They shew their love by their readiness to do his will, in the execution of which they fly as with wings, Ezek. 1:24, but you only have the happiness of testifying your love by your readiness to suffer for him, and is not this excellent?

Eighthly, When the heart is prepared for the worst sufferings, it is an argument that your will is subdued to the will of God; for till this be done, in a good measure, you cannot stand ready to suffer for him. But now, to have the will subdued by grace to the will of God, is a very choice and excellent frame indeed; for in this the main power of grace lieth: Look in what faculty the chief residence and strength of sin was, in the same chief residence the power of grace, after conversion, is also: Now it is in the will that the strength and power of sin (before conversion) lay. See John 5:40, Psa. 81:11, Jer. 44:16, 17. And indeed it was the devil's stronghold, which, in the day of Christ's power, he storms and reduces to his obedience, Psa. 110:3. O what a blessed thing is this! The will rules the man, it hath the empire of the whole man; it commands the faculties of the soul, *imperio politico*; and it commands the members of the body, *imperio despotico*.[1] Now to have Christ and grace

---

[1] *Imperio politico* = by an administrative order; *imperio despotico* = by an absolute order.

rule that which rules and commands your inner and outer man too, is no small mercy; and a better evidence that it is so cannot be given than this, that you stand ready, or do seriously prepare yourselves to suffer the hardest things for Christ: If your will can like that work, it is an argument grace hath conquered and subdued your wills indeed.

Ninthly, This preparation of heart to sufferings, is an excellent thing, because God is so abundantly pleased with it, that he often excuses them from sufferings in whom he finds it, and accepts it, as if the service had been actually done. So Abraham, Gen. 22:12, he was ready to offer up his Isaac's life to God; but God seeing his servant's heart really prepared, and ready for that difficult service, and high point of self-denial, provided himself another sacrifice instead of Isaac. Abraham shall have his son Isaac back again, and that with advantage; for he hath with him not only a choice experiment of his love to God, but God's high approbation of him, and acceptation of his offering. It was all one in respect of divine acceptance, as if he had been slain; and so the scripture represents it, James 2:21. And in this sense that promise is often made good to God's people who stand ready to give up their Isaacs, their lives, liberties, and dearest enjoyments to the Lord: 'He that will lose his life for my name's sake, shall save it,' Luke 9:24.

Now what a blessed thing is this! you may this way have the crown of martyrdom, and yet not shed one drop of blood for Christ actually. Ah! how kindly doth God accept it at his poor creatures' hands, when he sees how willing they are to serve him with their best enjoyments! 'It is well (saith he to David) that it was in thy heart,' 1 Kings 8:18.

Tenthly, And then, lastly, to add no more, it is beyond

controversy an excellent and blessed thing; because should such a Christian, after all his pains and preparations, be overborne, and fall by temptation: yet this preparation of his heart excuses his fall, from those aggravations that are upon the falls of others, and will give him both *support* under such a condition, and *encouragement* to hope for a speedy recovery out of it. Ah! it is no small comfort when a poor soul that hath been overborne by temptation, can come to God and say, 'Lord, thou knowest that this was not a wilful departure from my duty but contrary to the bent and resolutions of my heart; thou sawest my diligence beforehand to prepare for it; thou sawest my fears and tremblings of heart about it: O Lord, forgive, O Lord, recover thy servant, wash away this spot, it is one of the spots of thy children, an infirmity, not a rebellion': This may much stay the soul.

Surely, in this case, thou hast many grounds of comfort that another wants; for thy sin being but an infirmity, (1.) It is that which is common to all saints, Psa. 103:11-14. (2.) God hath mercy and pardons for such sins as these, else woe to the holiest soul, Psa. 130:3, 4. Solomon, upon this ground, pleads for mercy for them that prepared their hearts, 2 Chron. 30:18, 19. And God hath laid in sweet grounds of encouragement for such souls, Num. 15:27, 28, Heb. 5:2. How tenderly doth Christ deal with his disciples under this kind of sin, Matt. 26:41, and though they forsook him for a time, yet he received them again; though they fled from him, yet they all returned again and appeared boldly for Christ afterwards, and sealed their confession of him with their blood. And that which recovered them again was this, that their fall and departure was contrary to the resolution, and standing frame, and bent of their hearts;

for they resolved all to cleave to him to the death, Matt. 26:35, whereas those that engaged in a profession of him inconsiderately, and never resolved, nor prepared for the worst, fell off from him, and never returned any more, John 6:66. So then, upon the whole, you cannot but grant, that it is a very blessed and excellent thing, to prepare thus for the greatest suffering that can befall us for Christ. We come next to shew wherein it lies.

Chapter 5

Evincing the necessity of a sound and real work of grace upon the heart, to fit a man for suffering for Christ.

HAVING shewed you that God doth sometimes put his dearest people upon very hard services for him, and what an excellent thing it is to prepare ourselves to obey the call of God to them: In the next place I come to shew you, wherein this *preparation*, or *readiness* for suffering consists, and how many things concur and contribute their assistance to this work.

Now there is a twofold *preparation* or *readiness* for suffering; the one is *habitual*, the other *actual*: That *habitual readiness* is nothing else but the *inclination* of a soul to suffer any thing for Christ: which *inclination* ariseth from the principles of grace infused into the soul: But then as fire, though it have a natural inclination to ascend, yet may be violently depressed and hindered, that it cannot ascend actually, so may it be in this case; and therefore, before a man can be fitted for sufferings as Paul was, there must, to this habitual, be superadded an *actual readiness*, which is nothing else but the rousing of grace out of the sleepy and dull habits, and awakening it to its work in a time of need: as the lion is said to lash himself with his tail, to rouse up his courage before he fight. The former is a *remote* power, the latter a *proxim* and immediate power. I must handle the former in this chapter, and you are to know that it *consisteth in a sound and real work of grace or conversion wrought upon the soul*; without which I shall make it evidently appear to you, that no man can be fit or ready to suffer as a Christian.

Whatever stock of natural courage, moral principles, or common gifts of the Spirit be lodged in any man's breast, yet all this (without special grace) can never fit him to suffer for Christ. And had not this work been really and soundly wrought upon the heart of this blessed man, as indeed it was, Acts 9:3-5, he had quickly fainted under his sufferings: and so will every soul sooner or later do, that suffers not upon the same principles that he did.

1. For first, No man can suffer for Christ until he be able to deny himself. See Matt. 16:24. Self-denial goes in order of nature before sufferings. Beloved, in a suffering hour the interest of Christ and self meet like two men upon a narrow bridge, one must of necessity go back, or the other cannot pass on: If you cannot now deny *self* you must deny *Christ*. The yoke and dominion of *self* must be *cast off*, or else Christ's yoke and burden cannot be taken on.

It is confessed self may not only *consist with*, but be a *motive* to some kind of sufferings: Ambition and applause may carry a man far this way: pride is a *salamander* that it seems can live in the flames of martyrdom, 1 Cor. 13:3. But to be a *servant* to self and a true *sufferer* for Christ is incompatible. Self may make you the *devil's martyrs*, but grace only can make you *Christ's martyrs*. So that let a man be seemingly carried for a while with never so high a tide of zeal for Christ, yet if self be the spring that feeds, those self-ends, like so many little ditches joined to the brink of a river, will so suck and draw away the water into themselves, that the lofty stream will sink and come to nothing ere it have ran far: So then, of necessity, self must be dethroned in the hearts of Christ's suffering servants.

But now it is real grace only that disposes self, and subjects its interest to Christ's; for sanctification is nothing else but the *dethroning of exalted self, and the setting up of Christ's interest above it in the soul*. This is it that alters the property of all a man hath, and superscribes them with a new title, *Holiness to the Lord*, Isa. 23:18, Zech. 14:20, 21. Thenceforth a man looks at himself as none of his own, but past into another's right, 1 Cor. 6:19; and that he must neither *live*, nor *act ultimately* for himself, but for Christ, Rom. 14:7, Heb. 13:7, 8, Phil. 1:20. He is no more as a *proprietor*, but a steward of all he hath; and so holds upon these terms, to lay it out as may best serve his Master's ends and glory.

All that he is or hath, is by grace subordinated to Christ; and if once *subordinated*, then no more *opposed* to him, *subordinata non pugnant*.[1] This is it that makes him say, I care not what becomes of me or so Christ may be glorified, 'Let Christ be magnified in my body, whether it be by life or death,' Phil. 1:20.

By conversion Christ enters the soul, as an army doth an enemy's garrison by storm, and when he is possessed of it by grace, he presently divides the whole spoil of self betwixt himself and his church 2 Cor. 10:5. This is the first thing that evinces the necessity of a work of grace to prepare the heart for sufferings.

---

[1] 'Anything that is subordinated to someone does not fight against him.'

[49]

2. And then in the next place, it is as evident that a man can never be fit to suffer hard things for Christ until his spirit be enlarged raised, and ennobled, so that he be able to despise dangers, and look all difficulties in the face. That low and *private* spirit must be removed, and a *public* spirit must possess him. If a man be of a feeble and effeminate spirit, every petty danger will daunt and sink him; delicacy and tenderness is as unsuitable to a Christian as to a soldier, 2 Tim. 2:3. They that mean to enter into the kingdom of God, must resolve to make their way through that break of troubles betwixt them and it, 2 Tim. 3:12. They that will be crowned with victory, must stand to it, and play the men, as that word imports, 1 Cor. 16:13. Look over all the sacred and human histories, and see if you can find a man that ever honoured Christ by suffering, that was not of a raised and noble spirit, and in some measure able to contemn both the allurements and threats of men. So those three noble Jews Dan. 3:16, 17. So Moses, Heb. 11:27. And so our apostle, Acts 20:24. And the same heroic and brave spirit was found in the succeeding ages amongst the witnesses of Christ. When Valence the emperor endeavoured to draw Basil from the faith by offers of preferment, 'offer these things (saith he) to children'; when he threatened him with torments, 'threaten these things (saith he) to your purple gallants that live delicately.' And the same Basil relating the story of the forty martyrs, saith, That when great honours and preferments were offered them to draw them from Christ, their answer was, 'Why offer you these small things of the world to us (o emperor), when you know the whole world is contemned by us!' So Luther, money could not tempt him, nor the fear of man daunt him. 'Let me (said he in his letter

to Staupicius) be accounted proud, covetous, a murderer, guilty of all vices, rather than of wicked silence and cowardice in the cause of Christ.' Thus you see to what an height, and holy greatness, the spirits of suffering saints in all ages have been raised.

But now it is grace that thus raises the spirits of men above all the smiles and honours, frowns and fears of men; and no other principle but grace can do it. There is indeed a *natural stoutness* and generosity in some which may carry them far, as it is said of Alexander, that when any great danger approached him, his courage would rise, and he would say, *Jam periculum par animo Alexandri*; Here is a danger fit for Alexander to encounter: So Pompey, when dissuaded from a dangerous voyage, answered, *Necesse est ut eam, non ut vivam*. 'It is necessary that I go, not that I live.' But this being fed only by a natural spring, can carry a man no higher than nature, and will flag at last. If applause, and the observation of the world supply it not, it quickly ebbs and fails.

But as grace raises men much higher; so it maintains it even when there is nothing to encourage without; when forsaken of all creatures and visible supports, 2 Tim. 4:16. And this it doth three ways: (1.) By giving him that hath it a view of far greater things, which shrinks up all temporary things, and makes them appear but trifles and small matters, Rom. 8:18, 2 Cor 4:18. By grace a man rises with Christ, Col. 3:1. It sets him upon his high places, and thence he looks down upon things below as very poor and inconsiderable. The great cities of Campania seem but little spots to them that stand on the top of the Alps. (2.) By teaching him to value and measure all things by another thing than he was wont to do. He did once measure life, liberty, riches, honours by sense and time; and then they seemed great things, and it was hard to deny them, or thus to slight them; but now he values and measures all by faith and eternity; and esteems nothing great and excellent but what hath a reference to the glory of God, and an influence into eternity. (3.) Grace raises and ennobles the spirit thus, because it is the divine nature; it is the Spirit of Christ infused into a poor worm, which makes a strange alteration on him, transforms him into another manner of person; as much difference betwixt his spirit now and what it was, as betwixt the spirit of a child that is filled with small matters, and taken up with toys, and of a grave *statesman* that is daily employed about the grand affairs of a kingdom.

3. A man can never suffer as a Christian till his will be subjected to the will of God. He that suffers *involuntarily*, and out of necessity, not out of choice, shall neither have acceptance nor reward from God. Of necessity the will must be subjected; a man can never say, *Thy will be done*, till he can first say, *Not my will*.

But it is grace only that thus conquers and subjects the will of man to God's, Psa. 110:3. This is that which exalts God's authority in the soul, and makes the heart to stoop and tremble at his commands. It is that which makes our will to write its *fiat* at the foot of every command, and its *placet* under every order it receives from God. No sooner was grace entered into the soul of Paul, but presently he cries out, 'Lord, what wilt thou have me to do?' Acts 9:6. The will is to the soul what the wheels are to the chariot; and grace is to the will what oil is to those wheels. When we receive the Spirit of grace, we are said to *receive an unction from the Holy One*, 1 John 2:20. And when the soul is made as the chariots of Amminadib, Song of Sol. 6:12. *Non tardat uncta rota*,[1] it runs freely after the Lord, and cheerfully addresseth itself to the very service.

4. A man can never suffer as a Christian until his heart be composed, fixed, and determined to follow the Lord through all hazards and difficulties. As long as a man is hesitating and unresolved what to do, whether to go forward, or return back again to the prosperous world, when a man is at such a *pause*, and stand in his way, he is very unfit for sufferings. All such divisions do both *weaken* the soul, and *strengthen* the temptation: The devil's work is more than half done to his hand in such a soul, and he is now as unfit to endure hardship for Christ, as a ship is to ride out a storm that hath neither cable, anchor, nor ballast, to hold and settle it, but lies at the mercy of every wave, James 1:8, 'The double minded man is unstable in all his ways.' But it is grace, and nothing besides, that brings the heart to a fixed resolution and settlement to follow the Lord, it is grace that *establishes the heart*, Heb. 13:9, and unites it to fear the name of God, Psa. 86:11. This gathers all the streams into one channel, and then it runs with much strength, and sweeps away all obstacles before it. So that look as it is with a wicked man that hath sold himself to do wickedly, if he be set upon any one design of sin, he pours out his whole heart and strength into the prosecution of that design, which is the ground of that saying, *Liberet me Deus ab homine unius tantum negotii*, let God deliver me from a man of one only

[1] 'There is no delay when the wheels are properly oiled.'

design. He will do it to purpose: So is it also in grace; if the heart be composed, fixed, and fully resolved for God, nothing shall then stand before him. And herein lies much of a Christian's habitual fitness and ability to suffer.

5. The necessity of saving grace in all sufferers for Christ, will farther appear from this consideration, that he who will run all hazards for Christ, had need of a continual supply of strength and refreshment from time to time. He must not depend on anything that is failable; for what shall he do then when that stock is spent, and he hath no provision left to live upon? Now all natural qualifications, yea, all the common gifts of the Spirit, are failable and short-lived things; they are like a sweet flower in the bosom, that is an ornament for a little while, but withers presently: Or like a pond or brook occasioned by a great fall of rain, which quickly sinks and dries up, because it is not fed by springs in the bottom, as other fountain-waters are; and hence it is they cannot continue and hold out when sufferings come, Matt. 13:21. Because there is no root to nourish and support. The hypocrite will not always call upon God, Job 27:10. Though they may keep company with Christ a few miles in this dirty way, yet they must turn back at last, and shake hands eternally with him, John 6:66. These *comets* may seem to shine for a time among the stars, but when that earthly matter is spent, they must fall and lose their glory.

But now grace is an everlasting principle, it hath springs in the bottom that never fail. 'I shall be in him (saith Christ) a well of water springing up into eternal life,' John 4:14. The Spirit of God supplies it from time to time, as need requires. It hath daily incomes from heaven, 2 Cor. 1:5, Phil. 4:13, Col. 1:11. So that it is our union with Christ the Fountain of grace, that is the true ground of our constancy and long suffering.[1]

6. And then lastly, it will appear by this also, that there is an absolute necessity of a real change by grace on all that will suffer for Christ; because although we may engage ourselves in sufferings without it, yet we can never manage our sufferings like Christians without it. They will neither be honourable nor acceptable to God, nor yet beneficial and comfortable to ourselves or others, except they be performed from this principle of grace: For upon what principle soever beside this any man is acted in religion, it will either cause him to decline sufferings for Christ; or, if he be engaged in them, yet he will little credit religion by his sufferings. They will either be spoiled by an ill management, or his own pride will devour the praise and glory of them. I do not deny but a man that is graceless may suffer many hard things upon the account of his profession, and suffer them all in vain as these scriptures manifest. See 1 Cor. 13:3, Gal. 3:4. And although you may find many sweet promises made to those that suffer for Christ, yet must consider that those pure and spiritual ends and motives by which men ought to be acted in their sufferings, are always supposed and implied in all these promises that are made to the external action. And sometimes it is expressed, 1 Pet. 4:16. To suffer [as a Christian] is to suffer from pure Christian principles, and in a Christian manner, with *meekness, patience, self-denial*, etc. and this grace only can enable you

[1] We are only so far safe as we are united to Christ.

to do: So that by all this, I hope what I have undertaken in this character, viz. To evince the necessity of a work of grace to pass upon you, before sufferings for religion come, is performed to satisfaction.

Chapter 6

Wherein the nature of this work of grace, in which our habitual fitness for suffering lies, is briefly opened, and an account given of the great advantage the gracious person hath for any, even the hardest work thereby.

HAVING in the former chapter plainly evinced the necessity of saving grace to fit a man for sufferings; it will be expected now that some account be given you of the nature of the work, and how it advantages a man for the discharge of the hardest services in religion: Both which I shall open in this chapter by a distinct explication of the parts of this description of it.

This work of grace, of which I am here to speak, *consists in the real change of the whole man by the Spirit of God, whereby he is prepared for every good work*: In which brief description I shall open these four things to you,

1. That it is a change; that is palpably evident, both from scripture and experience, 2 Cor. 5:17, 'Old things are passed away; behold all things are become new'; and it is so sensible a change, that it is called *a turning from darkness to light*, Acts 26:18, and a new creature formed and brought forth. But to be a little more distinct and particular, there are several other changes that pass upon men, which must not be mistaken for this; and therefore, (1.) It is not a mere

change of the judgment from error to truth, from Paganism to Christianity. Such a change Simon Magus had, yet still remained in the gall of bitterness, and fast bound in the bonds of iniquity, Acts 8:23. (2.) Nor only of a man's practice, from *profaneness* to *civility*: This is common among such as live under the light of the gospel, which breaking into men's consciences, thwarts their lusts, and overawes them with the fears of hell: Which is no more than what the Gentiles had, Rom. 2:15. (3.) Nor is it a change from mere *morality* to mere *formality* in religion. Thus *hypocrites* are changed by the common gifts of the Spirit, illuminating their minds, and slightly touching their affections, Heb. 6:4, 5. (4.) Nor is it such a change as justification makes, which is relative, and only alters the state and condition, Rom. 5:1, 2. (5.) Lastly, It is not a change of the essence of a man; he remains essentially the same person still. But this change consists in the infusion of new habits of grace into the old faculties; which immediately depose sin from its dominion over the soul, and deliver up the soul into the hands and government of Christ, so that it lives no more to itself, but to Christ. This is that change whereof we speak: And this change (2.) I assert to be real, no fancy, no delusion; not a groundless conceit, but it is really existent, *extra mentem*,[1] whether you conceit it or not. Indeed the blind world would persuade us it is *suppositious* and *fantastic*; and that there is no such real difference betwixt one man and another as we affirm grace makes. And hence it is, that whosoever professeth it, is presently branded for a fanatic; and that scripture, Isa. 66:5, *Stand by thyself, I am holier than thou*, etc. clapped in their teeth in their absurd and perverse sense of it.

[1] 'outside the mind.'

But I shall briefly offer these seven things to your consideration, which will abundantly evince the reality of it, and at once both stop the slanderous mouths of ignorant men, and silence those atheistical surmises, which at any time Satan may inject into the hearts of God's own people touching this matter. And *first*, let it be considered, that the Spirit of God hath represented to us this work of grace under such names and notions in scripture, as if they had been chosen purposely to obviate this calumny. It is called a *creature*, Gal. 6:15, a *man*, 1 Pet. 3:4, a *new birth*, John 3:3, Christ formed in us, Gal. 4:12. All which express its reality, and that it is not a conceited thing. (2.) It appears to be real by the marvellous effects it hath upon a man, turning him both in judgment, will, affections, and practice, quite counter to what he was before. This is evident in that famous instance of Paul, Gal. 1:23, which is abundantly attested and sealed by the constant experience of all gracious souls that are witnesses of the truth hereof. (3.) A divine and Almighty power goes forth to produce and work it; and hence faith is said to be of the operation of God, Col. 2:12. Yea, that the same power which raised Jesus Christ from the dead, goes to the production of it, Eph. 1:19, 20. And if so, how much less than blasphemy is it, to call it a conceit or fancy? Doth God set on work his infinite power to beget a fancy, or raise an imagination? (4.) Conceits and whimsies abound most in men of weak reason: Children, and such as are cracked in their understandings, have most of them: Strength of reason banishes them, as the sun doth mists and vapours: But now the more rational any gracious person is, by so much the more he is fixed, settled, and satisfied in the grounds of religion: Yea, there is the highest and purest reason in religion; and when this change is wrought upon men, it is carried on in a rational way, Isa. 1:18, John 16:9. The Spirit overpowers the understanding with clear demonstrations, and silences all objections, pleas, and pretences to the contrary. (5.) It is a real thing, and gracious souls know it to be so; else so many thousands of the saints would never have suffered so many cruel torments and miseries, rather than forsake a fancy, and so save all. They have been so well satisfied of the reality of that which the world calls a fancy, that they have chosen rather to embrace the stake than deny it. The constancy of Christians, in cleaving to religion, was common to a *proverb* among the *heathen*; who when they would express the greatest difficulty, would say, 'You may as soon turn a Christian from Christ as do it.' Surely no wise man would sacrifice his liberty, estate, life, and all that is dear, for a conceit. (6.) Its reality appears in its uniformity in all those in whom it is wrought: *They have all obtained like precious faith*, 2 Pet. 1:1. *They are all changed into the same image*, 2 Cor. 3:18. Three thousand persons affected in one and the same manner at one sermon, Acts 2:37. Could one and the same conceit possess them altogether? Take two Christians that live a thousand miles distant from each other, that never heard of one another, let these persons be examined, and their reports compared, and see if they do not substantially agree, and whether as face answers face in the water, so their experiences do not answer one to the other? Which could never be, if it were a groundless conceit. (7.) And lastly, It is manifest it is a reality, and puts a real difference betwixt one and another, because God carries himself so differently towards them after their conversion; now he smiles, before he frowned; now they are under the promises, before they were under the threats and curses; and what a vast difference will he put betwixt the one and the other in that great day? See Matt. 25. Surely if these nominal Christians did but differ in conceit, not really from others, the righteous Judge of all the earth would not pass such a different judgment and doom upon them.

By all this you evidently see, that grace is a real change, and not a conceited one.

3. We say that this real change passes upon the whole man: he is changed in *soul*, *body*, and *practice*: all things are become new. (1.) This change appears in his soul: For by it, (1.) His understanding is strangely altered, and receive things in another way than formerly. It did look at Christ and things eternal as uncertain and light matters; the things that are seen and present do mostly affect, and appeared great and excellent: It admired riches and honour, whilst Christ and glory were overlooked and despised. But now all these temporals are esteemed dung, dross, vanity, Phil. 3:8, 11, Rom. 8:18. And Jesus Christ is now esteemed *the wisdom and the power of God*, 1 Cor. 1:23, 24. It did look on the saints as despicable persons, but now as the *excellent of the earth*, Psa. 16:3. Strictness and duty was once esteemed a needless thing, but now the only thing desirable, Psa. 119:14, 'Oh,' saith the renewed soul, 'where were mine eyes, that I could see no more excellency in Christ, his ways and people?' (2.) It stops not there (as it doth in hypocrites) but passes on further, and reduces the will; that stronghold is taken, and delivered up to Christ. It did rebel against God, and could not be subject, but now it submits, Acts 9:6, *Lord, what wilt thou have me to do?* In the day of Christ's power

he presents himself in all his drawing glory and loveliness before the will, and cries to that stubborn faculty, *Open to me, open to me*; with which word there goes forth an opening and subduing power, which the will no sooner feels, but it spontaneously moves towards him, and saith, *Stand open ye everlasting gates, that the King of glory may come in*. Henceforth it votes for God, subscribes and submits to his will as its only rule and law; and indeed it becomes the principal seat where grace makes its residence; and where, for the most part, it is more visible than in any other faculty. For after a man hath searched for it in all other faculties, and cannot discern it, yet here he ordinarily finds it; to will is present, Rom. 7:18. (3.) The will being thus gained to Christ, love comes in of course; it, feeling the power of grace also, presently changeth its object: It seizeth not so greedily on earthly objects as before, but is strangely cooled and deadened to them, by the appearance of a far greater glory in Jesus Christ; which hath so captivated the soul, and strongly attracted their affection, that it is now become very remiss in all its actings towards them; and often (especially at first) it is so weaned from all things on earth, that the temptation seems to lie on the other extreme, even in too great neglect of our lawful employments and comforts. Now Jesus Christ, Song of Sol. 1:3, his ordinances, Psa. 119:97, and his saints, 1 John 3:14, are the only delights and sweetest companions; he could sit from morning till night, to hear discourses of Christ his beloved, and could live and die in the company of his people, whose company is now most delightful and sweet, Psa. 119:63. (4.) The desires are altered, they pant no more after the dust of the earth, Psa. 4:6, but pant for God, as the *hart after the water brooks,*

Psa. 42:1. Yea, so big is the soul with them, that it is some-times ready to faint, yea, to break with the longing it hath after him, Psa. 119:20. (5.) The thoughts are changed, Psa. 119:113, and the thoughts of God are now most precious, Psa. 139:17, musing when alone of him; and in its solitudes the soul entertains itself with a delightful feast, which its thoughts of God bring in to refresh it, Psa. 63:5, 6. (6.) The designs and projects of the soul are changed; all are now swallowed up in one grand design, even to approve himself to God, and be accepted of him, 2 Cor. 5:9, and if he fail not there, it will not much trouble him, if all his other designs should be dashed. It were easy to instance in the rest of the affections, and shew how grace spreads and diffuses itself into them all, as light in the air, or leaven in the lump; but this may suffice, to shew how it passes upon the whole soul, and enters the several faculties and affections thereof.

And the soul being thus possessed for God, the body with all its members is consequently resigned up to him also: For the will hath the empire of the members of the body, as well as of the passions and affections of the soul. These are not any more delivered up to execute the lusts of Satan, but are yielded up to God for his ends and uses, Rom. 6:19. And thus you have the third thing in the description made out also, that it is an universal, as well as a real change. But then,

4. Lastly, You must know that by this change God prepares a man for choice and excellent services; and this indeed is the main thing designed in this chapter, and is the result and issue of all that hath hitherto been said about this work of grace.

Beloved, can you imagine that God could employ his infinite and glorious power to produce this new creature in such an excellent nature, it being the masterpiece of all his works of wonder wrought upon man, and not aim at some singular use and excellent end? Every wise agent designs some end; and what God aims at he hath told us, Isa. 43:21, Eph. 2:20. And accordingly he expects singular things from such persons, Matt. 5:48. If God had not aimed at some new service, he need not have made a new creature: the old creature was fit enough for the old use and service it was employed in. But God hath some choice service to be done wherein he will be glorified. He will have his name glorified, even in this world, by the active and passive obedience of his people. But this being far above all the power of nature, God therefore brings them forth in a new and heavenly nature, endowed with rare, supernatural, and divine qualities, by which it is fitted and excellently prepared for any service of God, by doing or by suffering, which before he had no fitness or ability for.

The very make and constitution of this new creature speaks its use and end: As now, if a man look upon a sword or knife (supposing he had never seen either before), yet, I say, by viewing the shape and properties of it, he will say, this was made to cut. Even so here, this new creature was formed for some glorious and singular service for God, to which it is exceedingly advantaged, whether God put you upon doing or suffering. If you ask wherein this advantage of the new creature to honour God either way lies; I answer, it principally consists in its *heavenly inclination*, or *natural tendency* to God. This is its great advantage; for, by virtue of this,

1. If God call a man to any duty, there is a *principle* within, closing with the *command* without, and moving the soul

freely and spontaneously to duty, Psa. 27:8, If God say, *Seek my face*, such an heart echoes to the call, *Thy face, Lord, will I seek*: And this is it which is called, *The writing of God's law in the heart*, Jer. 31:33, and must needs be a mighty advantage; for now its work is its delight and wages, Psa. 19:11. The command to such a soul is not grievous, 1 John 5:3, and by this it is kept from tiring in duty, and being weary of its work. As you see what pains children can take at play, how they will run and sweat, and endure knocks and falls, and take no notice of it; put them upon any manual labour, and they cannot endure half so much: When our work is our delight, we never faint not tire at it. This inclination to God is to the soul as wings to a bird, or sails to a ship. This carries the soul easily through every duty. O there is a vast difference betwixt a man that *works for wages*, and one whose *work is wages to him*. And here you may at once see wherein the principal difference betwixt the hypocrite and real Christian lies in the performance of duty; and also have a true account of the reason why one perseveres in his work to the end, when the other flags. Why, here is the true account of both; the one is moved to duty from a natural inclination to it, the other is forced upon it by some external motives: For the hypocrite takes not delight in the spiritual and inward part of duty, but is secretly weary of it, Mal. 1:13, only his ambition and self-ends put him upon it as a task. But now the upright heart goes to God as his joy, Psa. 63:4. And saith, 'It is good for me to draw nigh to God,' Psa. 73 *ult*. When the sabbath comes (*that golden spot of the week*), oh how he longs to *see the beauty of the Lord* in his ordinances! Psa. 27:4. And when engaged in the worship of God, he cannot satisfy himself in *bodily service*, or to serve God *in the oldness of the letter*. He knoweth that *this persuasion comes not of him that called him*, Gal. 5:7, 8. He labours to engage his heart to approach to God, Jer. 30:21. And hence those mountings of heart and violent sallies of the desires heavenward. And thus you see one rare advantage to glorify God actively, flowing from the inclination of this new creature.

2. But then, *secondly*, hence in like manner hath the soul as great an advantage for sufferings; for this new creature having such a natural tendency to God, will enable the soul in which it is, to break its way to God through all the interposing obstacles and discouragements. What are persecutions, what are reproaches, what are the fears and frowns of enemies, but so many blocks thrown into the soul's way to keep it from God and duty? And indeed where this principle of grace is wanting, they prove inaccessible mountains. Graceless hearts are stalled, and quite discouraged by them: but now this tendency of the soul to God enables the Christian to break his way through all. You may say of him in such a case as the historian doth of Hannibal (who forced a way over the Alps with fire and vinegar) either he will find a way, or make a way; 'Shall sword or famine, or any other creature separate me from Christ?' saith an upright soul. No, it will make its way through all to him, and that from this tendency of his new nature. You see in nature, everything hath a tendency to its centre; fire will up, do what you can to suppress it; water will to the sea; if it meet with dams, yea, mountains in its way, if it cannot bear them down, it will creep about some other way, and wind and turn to find a passage to the sea. God is the centre of

all gracious spirits, and grace will carry the soul through all to him. This is grace, and this is your advantage by it in the most difficult part of your work. It will carry you through all; make the hardest work easy and pleasant, 2 Cor. 12:10. And if great sufferings or temptations interpose betwixt you and your God, it will break through all, and enable you to withstand all; as it did Paul in the text, who forced his way not only through the fury of enemies, but also through the entreaties and tears of friends.

Chapter 7

*In which the necessity of getting clear evidences of this work
of grace in us, in order to our readiness for sufferings, is
held forth, the nature of that evidence opened; and divers
things that cloud and obscure it removed out of the way.*

I HAVE done with *habitual readiness*, consisting in an
in-wrought work of grace. The following particulars are
the things in which our *actual readiness* lies. And of them,
that which comes next to be handled, is the getting of
clear evidences in our own souls, that this work hath been
wrought in us: this will exceedingly tend to your strengthening and comfort in a suffering hour. Blessed Paul, who
here professeth himself ready both for bonds and death,
was clear in this point; 2 Tim. 1:12 and 4:6, 7. And indeed
had he been cloudy and dark in this, he could not have said,
I am ready. No, he had been in an ill case to undertake that
journey to Jerusalem: and thou wilt find it a singular advantage in dark and difficult days, to have all clear and right
within. Now, for the opening of this I will shew:

I. What the evidence or manifestation of the work of
grace is.

II. How it appears to be of such great advantage to a
suffering saint.

III. Prescribe some rules for the obtaining of it.

I. What it is. And, in short, it is nothing else but the *Spirit's shining upon his own work, in the hearts of believers, thereby enabling them sensibly to see and feel it to their own satisfaction.* And this is expressed in scripture under a pleasant variety of metaphors. Sometimes it is called the 'shedding abroad of the love of God in the heart,' Rom. 5:5. Sometimes 'the lifting up of the light of God's countenance,' Psa. 4:6, and sometimes it is expressed without a trope, by Christ's *manifesting himself* to the soul, John 14:21.

For the opening of it, I desire you would consider these six things.

1. That it is attainable by believers in this life, and that in a very high degree and measure. Many of the saints have had it in a full measure; 1 Cor. 2:12, John 4:24, John 21:15.

2. Though it be attainable by believers, yet it is a thing separable from true grace, and many precious souls have gone mourning for the want of it, Isa. 50:10. This was sometimes the case of Heman, David, Job, and multitudes more.

3. During its continuance it is the sweetest thing in the world. It swallows up all troubles, and doubles all other comforts: it puts more gladness into the heart, than the increase of corn and wine, Psa. 4:7. *Suavis hora, sed brevis mora; sapit quidem suavissime sed gustatur rarissime.*[1] Bernard.

4. Both in the continuation and removal of it the Spirit acts *arbitrarily.* No man can say how long he shall walk in this pleasant light, Psa. 30:7, 'By thy favour thou hast made my mountain stand strong: thou hidest thy face, and I was troubled.' And when in darkness, none can say how long

---

[1] 'The hour is sweet, but does not last long. The taste may be very sweet; but the experience is very infrequent.'

it will be ere that sweet light break forth again. God can scatter the cloud unexpectedly in a moment, Song of Sol. 3:4, 'It was but a little that I passed from them, but I found him whom my soul loveth.' There is such an observable difference in David's spirit in some Psalms, as if one man had written the beginning and another the end of them.

5. Though God can quickly remove the darkness and doubts of a soul, yet ordinarily the saints find it a very hard and difficult thing to obtain and preserve the evidences of their graces. Such is the darkness, deadness, and deceitfulness of the heart; so much unevenness and inconstancy in their practice, so many counterfeits of grace, and so many wiles and devices of Satan to rob them of their peace, that few (in comparison) live in a constant and quiet fruition of it.

6. Notwithstanding all these things, which increase the difficulty; yet God hath afforded his people a sure light, and sufficient means, in the diligent use of improvement whereof they may attain a certainty of the work of grace in them. And there is a threefold light by which it may most clearly and infallibly be discovered.

(1.) Scripture-light, which is able to discover the secrets of a man's heart to him; and is therefore compared to the Anatomizer's knife, Heb. 4:12.

(2.) The innate light of grace itself; or, if you will, the light of experience, 1 John 5:10. It hath some properties and operations which are as essential, necessary, and inseparable, as heat is to the fire, and may be as sensibly felt and perceived by the soul, Psa. 119:20.

(3.) The light of the Spirit, superadded to both the former, which is sometimes called its *earnest*, sometimes its *seal*. The Spirit doth but *plant* the *habits*, *excite* and draw forth the *acts*, and also *shine* upon his own work, that the soul may see it; and that sometimes with such a degree of light as only begets peace, and quiets the heart, though it doth not fully conquer all the doubts of it. And at other times the heart is irradiated with so clear a beam of light, that it is able to draw forth a triumphant conclusion, and say, Now I know the things that are freely given me of God: I believe, and am sure.

And so much briefly for the opening of the nature of this evidence.

II. I shall shew you the advantage of it to a suffering saint in order to the right management of a suffering condition.

And this will appear by the consideration of five things.

1. You will readily grant, that the Christian's love to God hath a mighty influence into all his sufferings for God. This grace of *love* enables him victoriously to break through all difficulties and discouragements. 'The floods cannot drown it, nor the waters quench it,' Song of Sol. 8:6, 7. It facilitates the greatest hardships, 1 John 5:3. And whatever a man suffers, if it be not from this principle it is neither acceptable to God, nor available to himself, 1 Cor. 13:3.

But now nothing more inflames and quickens the Christian's love to God, than the knowledge of his interest in him, and the sensible perception and taste of his love to the soul. Our love to God is but a reflection of his own love; and the more powerful the stroke of the direct beam is, the more is that of the reflex beam also. Never doth that *flame* of Jah burn with a more vehement heat, than when the soul hath the most clear manifestations of its interest in Christ and his benefits, Luke 7:47.

2. It must needs be of singular use to a suffering saint, because it takes out the sinking weight of affliction. That which sinks and breaks the spirit, is the conjunction and meeting of inward and outward troubles together; then if the Lord do not strangely and extraordinarily support the soul, it is wrecked and overwhelmed, as the ship in which Paul sailed was, when it fell into a place where two seas met, Acts 27:41. O how tempestuous a sea doth that soul fall in, that hath fightings *without*, and fears *within*! how must that poor Christian's heart tremble and meditate terror, that when he retires from troubles without, for some comfort and support within, shall find a sad *addition* to his troubles from whence he expected relief against them! hence it was that Jeremiah so earnestly deprecates such a misery, 'Be not thou a terror to me: thou art my hope in the day of evil,' Jer. 17:17. This is prevented by this means; if a man have a clear breast, and all be quiet within, he is like one that hath a good roof over his head when the storm falls. 'We glory in tribulation, because the love of God is shed abroad in our hearts,' Rom. 5:3, 5.

3. It is a fountain of joy and comfort in the darkest and saddest hour. Hence the glorious triumphs of saints in their afflictions, Rom. 5:5. And in the Christian's joy in the Lord, lies much of his strength for sufferings, Neh. 8:10. If once the spirit droops and sinks, the man is in a bad case to suffer: Holy joy, is the oil that makes the chariot-wheels of the soul free to follow the Lord, *Non tardat uncta rota.*[1] To suffer with joyfulness for Christ is a qualification that

[1] 'There is no delay when the wheels are properly oiled.'

God's eye is much upon in his suffering servants, Col. 1:11. How did the famous worthies that went before us magnify Christ, and glorify religion by the holy triumphs of their faith and joy under tribulation! one kissed the *apparitor* that brought him news of his condemnation, and was like a man transported with an excess of joy: Another upon the pronouncing of the sentence kneels down, and with hands and eyes lifted up, solemnly blesses God for such a day as that. Oh how is Christ magnified by this! and this cannot be until interest be cleared. It is true, the *faith of recumbency* gives the soul a secret support, and enables the Christian to *live*; but the *faith of evidence* keeps him *lively*, and prevents all those uncomfortable and uncomely sinkings and despondencies of spirit, 2 Cor. 4:16, 17, and therefore cannot but be of a singular use to a soul at such a time.

4. And, lastly, It is of special use to a Christian under sufferings, inasmuch as it enables him to repel the temptations that attend upon sufferings. Nothing sets a keener edge upon his indignation against unworthy compliances, than this. Indeed a poor cloudy and dubious Christian will be apt to catch at deliverance, though upon terms dishonourable to Christ; but he that is clear in point of interest, abhors compositions and capitulations upon unworthy terms and conditions, Heb. 11:35 and 10:34. He that sees the gain and reward of suffering, will think he is offered to his loss, when life and deliverance are set before him upon such hard terms as sin is.

And thus you see what influence it hath into a suffering condition.

III. In the next place I promised to prescribe some rules for the attaining of this evidence, and the dispelling of those doubts by which it is usually clouded in the souls of believers. And oh, that by the faithful use of them you may attain it, against a suffering day come upon you.

Rule 1. And the first rule I shall give you is this, make it your business to improve grace more; for the more *vigorous* it is, the more *evidential* it must needs be, 2 Pet. 1:5-11. Oft how much time have many Christians spent in inquiring after the lowest signs of sincerity, and what may consist with grace? Which had they spent in the diligent improvements of the means of grace, for the increasing of it, they would have found it a shorter cut to peace and comfort by much.

Rule 2. Mistake not the rule by which you are to try yourselves, lest you give a false judgment upon yourselves. Some are apt to make those things signs of grace, which are not; and when the falseness of them is detected, how is that poor soul plunged into doubts and fears, that leaned upon them? As now, if a man should conclude his sincerity from his diligence in attending on the word preached; this is but a *paralogism* (as the apostle calls it), James 1:22. By which a man deceiveth his own soul; For that which is a note or mark, must be proper to the thing notified, and not common to anything else. There are divers sorts of *marks*; some are *exclusive*, the principal use of which is to convince bold pretenders, and discover hypocrites; such is that, 1 Cor. 9:9. It is a most certain sign where these are, there is no grace; but yet it will not follow on the contrary, that where these are not, there is no grace. See Luke 18:11. Others are *inclusive*, the use of which is not so much for trying of the truth, as the strength and degrees of grace. As now, when faith is described by the *radiancy* of it, or by some of its heroic acts, and promises made to some raised degrees and operations of it; as that, Eph. 3:12 etc., here a mistake is easily made. Besides those, or rather betwixt these, are another sort of marks, which are called positive marks: and these agreeing in the lowest degree of grace, are for the trial of the truth and sincerity of it. Such are these, 1 John 4:13, 1 John 2:3, Matt. 5:3. Be sure to try by a proper mark.

Rule 3. Take heed of such sins as violate and waste the conscience; for these will quickly raise a mist, and involve the soul in clouds and darkness, Psa. 51:8, etc. Such are sins against light, and the reclamations of conscience.

Rule 4. Labour to shun those common mistakes that Christians make in judging of their state; among which I shall select these five as principal ones.

(1.) Call not your condition into question upon every failing and involuntary lapse into sin. 'Iniquities prevail against me: as for our transgressions, thou shalt purge them away,' Psa. 65:3. In short, thou needest not call thy condition into question, provided thou find thy spirit working as Paul's did under the surprisals of temptations: viz. If, (i.) Thou do approve of and delight in the law, though thou fall short of it in thy practice, Rom. 7:12, 14. (ii.) If thy failings be involuntary, and against the resolution and bent of thy soul, verses 15, 18, 19. (iii.) If it be the load and burden of thy soul, verse 24. (iv.) If the thoughts of deliverance comfort thee, verse 25.

(2.) Question not the truth of thy grace, because it was not wrought in the same way and manner in thee, as in others: For there is a great variety, as to the circumstances of *time* and *manner*, betwixt the Spirit's operations upon one and another. Compare the history of Paul's conversion with that of the jailor, Zaccheus, or Lydia, and see the variety of circumstances.

(3.) Conclude not that you have no grace, because you feel not those transports and ravishing joys that other Christians speak of. If thou canst not say as Paul doth, Rom. 8:38, yet bless God, if thou canst but breathe forth such language as that, Mark 9:24, 'Lord, I believe; help thou my unbelief.'

(4.) Say not thou hast no grace, because of the high attainments of some hypocrites, who in some things may excel thee. When some persons read the sixth chapter to the Hebrews, they are startled to see to what a glorious height the hypocrite may soar; not considering that there are these three things wherein they excel the most glorious hypocrite in the world. (i.) That self was never dethroned in hypocrites, as it is in them. All that an hypocrite doth is for himself. (ii.) The hypocrite never hated every sin, as he doth; but hath still some Agag, Rimmon, or Delilah. (iii.) That the hypocrite never acted in duty from the bent and inclination of a new nature, taking delight in heavenly employment, but is moved rather as a clock by the weight and poises of some external motives and advantages.

(5.) Conclude not you have no grace, because you grow not so sensibly as some other Christians do. You may be divers ways mistaken about this. (i.) You may measure your growth by your desires, and then it appears nothing; for the Christian aims high, and grasps at all. (ii.) Or by comparing yourselves with such as have larger capacities, time, and advantages than you. (iii.) Or by comparing your graces with other men's gifts, which you mistake for their graces.

(iv.) Or by thinking that all growth is upward in joy, peace, and comfort; whereas you may grow in mortification and humility, which is as true a growth as the former. Oh! take heed of these mistakes; they have been very prejudicial to the peace of many Christians.

Rule 5. Lastly, Decline not sufferings when God gives you a fair call to them. Oh! the Christian's suffering time is commonly his clearest and most comfortable time. 'Then the Spirit of God and glory resteth on them,' 1 Pet. 4:14. That which hath been in suspense for some years, is decided and cleared in a suffering hour. And thus I have shewed you how to *attain this necessary qualification also.*

Chapter 8

Discovering the necessity of an improved faith for the right management of sufferings, and directing to some special means for the improvement thereof.

THE next thing conducing to our actual readiness for sufferings, is the improvement of faith to some considerable degree of strength. This is the grace that must do the main service in such an hour, and hath the principal hand in supporting the Christian under every burden. This is the grace that crowns our heads with victory in the day of battle, Eph. 6:16, 'Above all, taking the shield of faith.' It is true every grace is of use, and contributes assistance: Suffering saints have been beholding to them all. But of this we may say, as Solomon of the virtuous woman; 'Though many graces have done excellently, yet this excels them all.' In this grace Paul was very eminent; it was the life he daily lived, Gal. 2:20. Oh! it is a precious grace, 2 Pet. 1:1. So precious, that Christ, who seldom admired anything, yet wondered at this, Matt. 8:10. A victorious grace it is that overcomes all difficulties, Mark 9:23. By this sword it was that all those famous *heroes*, Heb. 11, achieved all those glorious conquests; and in every distress it may say to the soul, as Christ to the disciples, John 15:5, 'Without me ye can do nothing.' This is that *sword* that hath obtained so many victories over the world, 1 John 5:4. And that trusty *shield* that hath quenched so many deadly darts of temptation, which have been levelled at the very heart of a Christian in the day of battle. By it a Christian lives, when all outward, sensible comforts die, Hab. 2:4. It is the ground upon which the Christian fixes his foot, and never fails under him, 2 Cor. 1:24. The necessity of it will more clearly appear, by considering how many ways it relieves the soul in trouble, and disburdens the heart of all its sinking loads and pressures: There are two things that sink a man's spirit when under sufferings: viz. The *greatness* of the troubles, and the *weakness* of the soul to bear them; against both which faith relieves the soul, viz. by making a *weak* soul *strong*, and *heavy* troubles *light*.

First, It makes a weak soul strong and able to bear; and this it doth divers ways.

1. By purging out of the soul those enfeebling and weakening distempers: not only *guilt* in general, which is to the soul as a wound upon the bearing shoulder, Rom. 5:1. The removal whereof enables the soul to bear any other burden, Isa. 33:24. But it also removes *fear*, that tyrant passion, that cuts the nerves of the soul. For as *faith* comes in, so *fear* goes out: Look in what degree the fear of God is ascendent in the soul, proportionably the sinful fear of the creature declines and vanisheth, Isa. 8:12, 13. This fear extinguishes that, as the sunshine puts out fire, 'The righteous is bold as a lion,' Prov. 28:1. The word כְּפִיר [*kephir*] signifies a young lion in his hot blood, that knows no such thing as fear! And look, how much of the soul is *empty* of faith, so much it is *filled* with fear: 'Why are ye fearful, O ye of little faith?' Matt. 8:26. Certainly, it is a rare advantage, to be freed from

the *common distraction*, in times of *common destruction*; and this advantage the soul hath by faith.

2. It strengthens the soul to bear afflictions and hardships; not only by purging out its weakening distempers, but by turning itself to Christ, in whom all its strength lies; and that suitably to the several exigencies of the soul in all its distresses. Doth darkness, like the shadow of death overspread the earth, and all the lights of earthly comforts disappear? then faith supports the heart by looking to the Lord, Micah 7:7. And this look of faith exceedingly revives the heart, Psa. 34:5, and enlightens the soul. Doth God pluck away all earthly props from under your feet, and leave you nothing visible to rest upon? in that exigence faith puts forth a suitable act, viz. *Resting* or *staying upon God*, Isa. 26:3, and by this the soul comes to be quieted and established, Psa. 125:1. Do temptations strive to put off the soul from Christ, and discourage it from leaning upon the promise? Then it puts forth *an act of resolution*, Job 13:15. And so breaks its way through that discouragement; or hath the soul been long seeking God for deliverance out of trouble, and still there is silence in heaven, no answer comes; but instead of an answer comes a temptation, to throw up the duty, and seek to deliver itself? Then faith puts forth another act upon Christ, suitable to this distress, viz. *An act of waiting*, Isa. 49:23, which waiting is opposed to that *sinful haste* which the soul is tempted to, Isa. 28:16. Or doth God at any time call the soul forth to some difficult service, against which the flesh and carnal reason dispute and plead? Now faith helps the soul, by putting forth *an act of obedience*; and that whilst carnal reason stands by dissatisfied, Gal. 1:16. And hence it is, that obedience carries the name of faith upon it

to shew its descent, Rom. 16:26. Faith encourages the soul to obey, not only by urging God's *command*, but by giving it God's *warrant* for its indemnity, Heb. 11:24-26. Or doth a poor believer find himself overmatched by troubles and temptations, and his own inherent strength begin to fail under the burden? Then faith leads him to an omnipotent God, and so secures him from fainting under his trouble, Psa. 61:2. In the Lord is everlasting strength. *El Shaddai* is a name of an encouragement to a feeble soul, Isa. 40:29-31. And thus you see the first particular made good, viz. What a strengthening influence it hath upon a weak soul.

Secondly, In the next place let us see how it *lightens* the Christian's burdens, as well as *strengthens* his back to bear.

And certainly, this grace of faith doth strangely alter the very nature of sufferings, taking away both the *heaviness* and *horror* of them; and this it doth divers ways:

1. By committing the business to Christ, and leaving the matter with him; and so quitting the soul of all these anxieties and perturbations, which are the very burden and weight of affliction, Psa. 37:5. For certainly that which sinks us in days of trouble, is rather from within, from our unruly, seditious, and clamorous thoughts, than from the troubles themselves with which we conflict: But by committing the matter to God, the soul is quickly brought to rest.

2. By discovering much present good in our troubles; the more good faith discovers in a trouble, the more supportable and easy it makes it to the soul. Now faith brings in a comfortable report, that they are not *only evils*, as the troubles of the wicked are, Ezek. 7:5, but have an allay and mixture of much good, Heb. 12:10, Isa. 27:9.

3. By foreseeing the end and final removal of them, and that near at hand, 2 Cor. 4:17. That which daunts and amazes men in times of trouble is, that they can see no end of them. Hence the heart faints, and hands hang down through discouragement: But now faith brings the joyful tidings of the end of troubles; and saith to the soul, 'Why art thou cast down, O my soul? and why so disquieted and discouraged within me? as if thy sufferings were like the sufferings of the damned, endless and everlasting, whereas they are but for a moment; yet a little while, a very little while, and he that shall come will come, and will not tarry,' Heb. 10:37. Yet a little while, and then the days of thy mourning shall be over.

4. By comparing our sufferings with the sufferings of others, which exceedingly diminisheth and shrinks them up; sometimes the believer compares his sufferings with Christ's, and then he is ashamed that ever he should complain and droop under them. Oh! saith he, what is that to that which the Lord Jesus suffered for me? He suffered in all his *members*, head, hands, side, feet, from all *hands*, friends and enemies, in all his *offices*; yea, in his soul, as well as in his body: And indeed the sufferings of his soul were the very soul of his sufferings: Sometimes he compares them with the sufferings of others of the saints in former ages: When he reads in faith the history of their persecutions, he is shamed out of his complaints, and saith, 'Am I better than my fathers?' Sometimes he compares them with the sufferings of the damned: 'O what is this to everlasting burnings! What is a prison to hell? How light and easy is it to suffer for Christ, in comparison of those sufferings which are from Christ?' And thus the soul is quieted, and the terror of sufferings abated.

5. Faith entitles Christ to the believer's sufferings, and puts them upon his score; and so it exceedingly transforms and alters them: Ah! it is no small relief when a man can hold up the Bible, as that *martyr* did at the stake, and say, 'This is that which hath brought me hither': Or as the Psalmist; 'For thy sake we are killed all the day long'; Or as the apostle, Col. 1:24, 'I fill up that which is behind of the sufferings of Christ in my flesh.'

6. Lastly, Faith engages the presence of God, to be and abide with the soul in all its solitudes and sufferings: It lays hold upon the promises made to that purpose, Psa. 23:2, Isa. 43:2, Heb.13:5, John 14:18. And whilst a poor soul enjoys this the very sense of troubles is swallowed up.

And thus I have given some brief hints how faith relieves and strengthens the soul in a suffering hour: The next thing is to direct you how to improve this excellent grace, that it may do you such service as this in a time of need: And, in order thereunto, I shall give you these seven directions.

Direction 1. Attend diligently upon the ministration of the gospel, which is not only the procreant, but also the conserving cause of faith, 1 Pet. 2:2. The *doctrine of faith* is the food and nutriment of the *grace of faith*: There are its rules, its encouragements, its cordials: Thence faith takes and treasures up its *michtams*, to which it hath recourse in times of need: Every *attribute, command*, or *promise* that shines forth there, is a dish for faith to feed on; but all together are a royal feast, Psa. 63:5. Some say the land of Judea, is called *the land of the living*, in Psa. 27:13, in respect of the ordinances of God which that people enjoyed. Certain it is, they are the great instruments of quickening souls at first, and preserving that life it so begat in them: But then be sure they have Christ's stamp upon them, and that they be ministered by his own officers, and in his own way: And so you may reasonably expect more fruits and influences from them than from all private gifts and helps in the world: 'For the Lord loveth the gates of Zion more than all the dwellings of Jacob,' Psa. 87:2. And all private helps may say, in comparison of Christ's public ordinances, as Gideon said to the men of Ephraim, Judg. 8:2, 'What have we done in comparison of you?'

Direction 2. Improve well your sacrament seasons, those harvest days of faith: This ordinance hath a direct and peculiar tendency to the improvement and strengthening of faith. It is a pledge superadded to the promise for faith's sake: Heavenly and sublime mysteries do therein stoop down to your senses, that you may have the clearer apprehensions of them; and the clearer the apprehensions are, the stronger the assent of faith must needs be: By this seal also the promise comes to be more ratified to us; and the firmer the promise appears to the soul, the more bold and adventurous faith is in casting itself upon it; Oh! how many poor, doubting, trembling souls have, in such a season, gathered the full ripe fruits of assurance from the top boughs of that ordinance!

Direction 3. Frequent actings of faith are rare and special means of improving it: *To him that hath*, i.e. that improves and uses what he hath, *shall be given*, Matt. 25:29. This was the way by which Paul thrived in faith and every other grace so exceedingly, that he outgrew them that were in Christ before him, 1 Cor. 15:10. It is true, its beginning in the soul is not after the manner of other habits, either moral or natural: This is not of natural acquisition, but by divine infusion: But yet its improvement is in the same manner. Oh then! if ever you would have a flourishing faith, rouse it up out of the dull habit, and live in the daily exercise of it.

Direction 4. Go to Jesus Christ, who is the Author and finisher of faith, and cry to him, as Mark 9:24, *Lord, increase my faith*: Yea, beg the assistance of others' prayers in this behalf, as the apostle did, 1 Thess. 3:10, 2 Thess. 1:11, faith animates prayer, and prayer increaseth faith.

Direction 5. Improve times of affliction for the increase of faith: For certainly, sanctified afflictions do notably exercise and increase this grace, 1 Pet. 1:7. In times of prosperity we know not what stock of faith we have: We live so much upon things seen, that we cannot many times tell whether we have faith or no: But when difficult days come, then we must get out our whole subsistence and livelihood by faith, Hab. 2:4. Yea, then we have many proofs and experiments of God's fidelity in the promises, which is a choice help to faith, 2 Cor. 1:10.

Direction 6. Keep catalogues of all your remarkable experiences; treasure them up as food to your faith in time to come: Oh! it is a singular encouragement and heartening to faith, when it can turn over the records of God's dealing with you in years past, and say as Joshua, *Not one thing hath failed*, Joshua 23:14. When it can say so of promises that have already had their accomplishments, then they will be apt to say concerning those yet to be accomplished, as Elisabeth said to Mary, Luke 1:45, 'Blessed is the soul that believeth, for there shall be a performance of those things which are told it by the Lord.'

These experiments are the food of faith, Psa. 74:14, 'Thou breakest the heads of Leviathan in pieces, and gavest him to be meat to the people inhabiting the wilderness,' i.e. That famous experience of the power and love of God in their Red Sea deliverance, where he destroyed that sea monster Pharaoh, and his host, was meat to the faith of God's Israel in the wilderness afterwards. We often find Christ charging the people's unbelief on a bad memory, Matt. 16:8, 9. And hence it was that the Lord commanded the Israelites to keep *journals* of every day's *occurrences*, Num. 33:1, 2. It is a thousand pities such choice helps should be lost. Oh! if you could but remember, how the Lord hath appeared for you in former exigencies, and how often he hath shamed you for your unbelief, it would exceedingly animate your faith, both in present and future distress, Micah 6:5.

Direction 7. Lastly, Beware of sense, which is the supplanter of faith. O if you live upon things earthly, you put your faith out of its office: Things earthly have an enmity to faith. 'This is the victory by which we overcome the world, even our faith,' 1 John 5:4. Overcoming denotes a conflict, and conflicts infer oppositions. Oh you that live so much by sight and sense on things visible, what will you do when in David's, or Paul's case, Psa. 142:4, 2 Tim. 4:16, when all outward encouragements and stays shall utterly fail? What had Abraham done if he had not been able to believe against hope, i.e. such an hope as is founded on sense and reason.

Reader, I advise and charge thee in the name of the Lord, and as thou hopest to live when visible comforts die, that thou be diligent in the improvement and preparation of this excellent grace of faith: if it fail, thou failest with it; and as thy faith is, so art thou. Consult also the cloud of witnesses, and see if thou canst find a man amongst them that did not achieve the victory by his faith. Had they not all been run down by the furious assaults of temptation, and instead of a *cloud of witnesses*, been so many *pillars of salt*, and monuments of reproach and shame to religion, if their faith had failed in its trial.

Chapter 9

Wherein the necessity and usefulness of Christian fortitude in order to sufferings is evinced, with a brief account of its nature and the means of attaining it.

THE next grace which occurs to the completing of our actual readiness for sufferings, is *Christian fortitude*, or holy courage; which must say in thy heart in a time of danger, as Elijah once did, 'As the Lord lives I will shew myself.' This also is a choice part of your preparation work. In this grace our apostle was eminent: when he was told, 'Bonds and afflictions waited for him'; he could say, That 'none of these things moved him,' Acts 20:24. Yea, when he was to appear before the lion Nero, and not a man would own or stand by him, yet he stands his ground, resolving rather to die on the place, than dishonourably to recede from his principles and profession, 2 Tim. 4:16, 17. He set the world, with all its threats and terrors lower than it set him. O how conspicuous was this grace in all those *heroes* that have passed on before us: And if ever you hope to stand in the evil day, and be fetched off the field with honour, you must rouse up and awaken your courage for God: And the necessity thereof will appear upon these four considerations.

1. Because the success and prevalence of Satan's temptations in the hour of persecution depends upon the fainting and overthrow of this grace. Wherefore doth he

raise persecutions in the world, but because such terrible things are fitted to work upon the passion of carnal fear, which rises with those dangers, and makes the soul as a tumultuous sea. This is it he aims at, Neh. 6:13. This is a multiplying passion that represents dangers more and greater than they are, and so drives the soul into the very net and snare laid by the devil to take it. Prov. 29:25, 'The fear of man brings a snare'; which was sadly exemplified in Abraham, Gen. 12:12, and divers others of the saints. If he can but subdue this grace, he will quickly bring you to capitulate for life and liberty, upon the basest and most dishonourable terms; therefore the preparation of this grace is so exceedingly necessary.

2. Because this is the grace that honours Jesus Christ abundantly, when you are brought upon the stage for him.

There is a great solemnity at the suffering and trial of a saint: heaven, earth, and hell, are spectators, observing the issue, and how the saints will acquit themselves in that hour. *We are made a spectacle*, saith the apostle. The word is θέατρον ἐγενήθημεν [*theatron egeneitheimen*], we are as set upon a theatre in public view, 1 Cor. 4:9. God, angels, and saints wait to see the glorious triumphs of their faith and courage, reflecting honour upon the name and cause of Christ. Devils and wicked men gape for an advantage by their cowardice. Certainly very much lies now upon the Christian's hands. Should he faint and give ground, how will it furnish the triumphs of hell, and make Christ's enemies vaunt over him, as if his love ran so low in the hearts of his people, that they durst not adventure anything for him? Or, as if, notwithstanding their brave words and glorious profession, they durst not trust their own principles when it comes to the trial: But if now they play the men, and discover an holy gallantry of spirit and resolution for Christ, how will it daunt the enemies, and make them say as Marcus, bishop of Aretheusa made one of Julian's nobles, present at his torments, to say concerning him, *We are ashamed, O emperor, the Christians laugh at thy cruelty!* And how will God himself rejoice and glory over them, as he once did over Job when he fetched him with honour off that first field! Job 2:3, 'Still he holdeth fast his integrity.'

3. Your own peace is wrapped up in it, as well as God's glory. Is it nothing, think you, to be freed from those *vultures* and *harpies* that feed upon the hearts of men at such times? Surely God reckons, that he promiseth a very great mercy to his people when he promiseth it. Prov. 1 *ult*, Psa. 112:7. When Borromaeus was told of some that lay in wait to take away his life, it troubled him not, but he said, *An Deus est in mundo pro nihilo?* What, is God in the world for nought? And like to this was the answer of Silentiarius in the like case; *Si Deus mei curam non habet, quid vivo?* If God take not care for me, how do I live? Oh this is it that brings you to an holy quietude of spirit in times of confusion and distraction, which is a choice mercy.

4. Your magnanimity is of special use to other saints, who are following you in the same path of sufferings. If you faint, it is like the fainting of a standard-bearer in an army: you bring thereby an evil report upon the cross of Christ, as the *first spies* did upon the land of Canaan. And a like influence with that it is like to have on your brethren; so that there is a necessity of improving this grace also before you can say with Paul you are ready.

Secondly, But what is this Christian fortitude, and wherein doth it consist?

I answer briefly, *It is an holy boldness in the performance of difficult duties, flowing from faith in the call of God, and his promise to us in the discharge of them.*

And so you have the nature of it in these four particulars:

1. It is an *holy boldness*, not a natural or sinful boldness, arising either from the natural constitution, or evil disposition of the mind.

2. It is expressed about duties for truth, not error, Jer. 9:3, for the interest of Christ, not of the flesh.

3. The season in which it appears is, when duties are surrounded and beset with difficulties and dangers, Dan. 3:16, 6:10.

4. The fountain whence it flows is faith, and that as it respects the command and call of God to duty, Acts 16:10. And his promise to us in the discharge thereof, Josh. 1:5, 6.

And his grace stands opposed both to the fear of man in the cause of God, Heb. 11:27, and to apostasy from the truth for fear of suffering. Thus briefly of the nature of it.

Thirdly, In the last place I shall lay down some rules for the promoting and improvement of it, and so finish this chapter.

Now there are ten rules heedfully to be observed for the breeding of holy courage in the breast of a saint in evil times.

Rule 1. And the first rule is this, Get a weaned heart from all earthly enjoyments. If the heart be inordinately fixed upon any one thing that you possess in the world, that inordinate estimation of, and affection for it, will strangely effeminate, soften, and cowardize your spirit when your trial comes, 2 Tim. 2:4. You meet not with a man of courage for God, but had his heart dead to earthly things; so it was with Paul, Phil. 3:8. Since the apostles, we scarce meet with a greater example of magnanimity than Luther; and if you read his story, you will find few men ever set a lower rate on the world than he. All the Turkish *empire* in his eye was but a crumb cast to the dogs. *Germana est haec bestia; pecuniam non curat.*[1] Money could not tempt him.

Rule 2. Suffer not guilt to lie upon your consciences: it is a fountain of fears, and you can never attain boldness for God till it be removed, Rom. 5:1-3. *The spirit of a sound mind* is opposed to the spirit of fear, 2 Tim. 1:7. Now that sound mind is a mind or spirit that is not wounded, and made sick and infirm by guilt. O what black fogs and mists arise out of guilt, which becloud our evidences, and fill us with fear and discouragements! Gen. 42:21, 22.

Rule 3. Clear your call to difficult services, be well satisfied that you are in that way and posture God expects to find you in. O what courage this will give! Josh. 1:9. Then a man may promise himself God's presence and protection, 2 Chron. 15:2. But whilst a man is dubious here, and cannot tell whether it be his duty or not that he is engaging in, how can he have courage to hazard anything for it? For thinks he, I may suffer much from men, and yet have no thanks of God for it, 1 Pet. 2:20. And further, till a man be clear in this, he cannot commit his cause to God. And it is a sad thing to be cut off from so choice a relief as that is, 1 Pet. 4:19.

Rule 4. Get right notions and apprehensions of your enemies. We are apt to *magnify* the creature, as if he could

[1] 'This beast is German; he does not care for money.'

do more than he *can*, and thereby *disable* ourselves from doing what we *should*. Possess your souls with the belief of these five things concerning them. (1.) That they are poor weak enemies, Isa. 40:15, 17, 22. But as a swarm of gnats in the air. See how God describes them, Isa. 51:13, 14. (2.) That little power they have is limited by your God who hath the bounding and ordering of it, John 19:11, Psa. 74:10. (3.) They carry guilt upon them, which makes them more timorous than you, Isa. 8:12. Their fear is a strange fear. (4.) They only use carnal weapons against you, which cannot touch your souls. If they were praying enemies that could engage God against you, they would be formidable enemies indeed; but this they cannot do. The largest commission that any of them ever had from God, extended but to the bodies and bodily concernment of the saints, Luke 11:4, 5. They cannot thunder with an arm like God, nor blot your name out of the book of life, nor take your part out of the *New Jerusalem*; therefore fear not man. (5.) Your enemies are God's enemies; and God hath espoused your cause and quarrel. The more cruel they are, the kinder he will be to you, John 9:34, 35.

Rule 5. Labour to engage the presence of God with you in all places and conditions. Whilst you enjoy this, your spirits will be invincible and undaunted, Josh. 1:9, Psa. 118:6. A weak creature assisted and encouraged by the presence of a great God will be able to do and suffer great things. Poor flesh in the hand of an almighty Spirit acts above itself. A little dog, if his master be by, and animates him, will seize upon a greater beast than himself, though he would run from him were his master absent. Our courage ebbs and flows as the manifestations of the divine presence do. Oh get thyself once within the line of that promise, Isa. 43:1, 2, and thou art invincible.

Rule 6. Get an high estimation of Jesus Christ, and all his concernments. They that *value* him *highest*, will *adventure* for him *farthest*. Magnanimous Luther, how inestimable a value did he set upon the truths of Christ! *Ruat coelum,* etc. *Let heaven rush rather than a crumb of truth should perish.* Thou wilt never be a man of zeal and courage for Christ's interest, until that interest of Christ have swallowed up all thine own interests. No sooner is the soul acquainted with, and interested in Christ, but he heartily wishes well to all his affairs and concernments, Psa. 45:3, 4. This is that which puts metal and resolution for Christ into the soul.

Rule 7. Beware you be not cheated with maxims of carnal policy, mistaken for Christian prudence. Many are so: and they prove destructive to all true zeal and courage for Christ. Never was religion professed with greater plainness and simplicity, than by the primitive Christians; and never was there an higher spring tide of courage and zeal for God, than in those days. We are apt to call it prodigality, and are grown wiser to husband our lives and comforts, better than they did. But indeed our prudentials have even swallowed up our religion. It is true, there is such a thing as Christian prudence; but this doth not teach men to shun all costly and difficult duties, and prostitute conscience to save the skin, 'A man of understanding walketh uprightly,' Prov. 15:21.

Rule 8. Look upon the inside of troubles for Christ, as well as upon the outside of them. If you view them by an eye of sense, there appeareth nothing but matter of discouragement. To look on the outside of a prison, banishment or death, is affrighting and horrible: but then if you look into the inside of these things by faith, and see what God hath made them to his people, and how joyful and comfortable they have been in these conditions; what honey they have found in the carcase of a lion, what songs in the stocks and dungeons, what glorying in tribulation, and hundredfold reward even in their sufferings: O then! that which looked like a serpent at a distance, will appear but as a rod in hand. How many have found themselves quite mistaken in their apprehensions of sufferings; and been more loath to come out of a prison, than they were to go in! If you did but see your supports and the comforts that souls ordinarily meet with in their troubles for Christ, you would not look on them as such formidable things.

Rule 9. View the issue and reward of sufferings by an eye of faith: this also will strongly abate the horror and dread of them, Heb. 10:34. Upon this account it is the saints have so slighted and contemned them, Rom. 8:18, 2 Cor. 4:16, 17. But then see that you act your faith, (1.) Upon the certainty of it: look at it as a most real and substantial thing, Heb. 11:1. (2.) View it as a great and *glorious reward*; And, (3.) As near at hand: And then say to thy soul, come on my soul, come on; seest thou the joy set before thee! the crown of glory ready to be set on thy head by the hand of a righteous God. Oh, what comparison is there betwixt those sufferings, and that glory!

Rule 10. Propound to yourselves the best patterns and examples. Keep your eye upon the cloud of witnesses; these are of special use to beget holy courage, Heb. 12:1, James 5:10. Who would be afraid to enter the lists, and grapple with that enemy that he hath seen so often foiled, and that by a poor weak Christian? See how the enemy with whom you are to grapple, hath been beaten hand to hand, and triumphed over by poor women and children; they had as great infirmities, and you have as gracious assistances as those that are gone before you.

Chapter 10

Discovering the necessity of an heart mortified to all earthly and temporal enjoyments, in order to the right managing of a suffering condition; with several directions for the attaining thereof.

THE next thing wherein your actual readiness for bonds, or death consisteth, is in *the mortification of your affections to all earthly interest and enjoyments; even the best and sweetest of them.* Till this be done, in some measure, you are not fit to be used in any such service for the Lord, 2 Tim. 2:21. The living world is the very life of temptations: the travailing pains of death are stronger and sharper upon none, than those that are full of sense and self. As you see in nature, what conflicts and agonies strong and lively persons suffer when they die; when others, in whom nature is decayed and spent beforehand, die away without half that pain, even as a bird in a shell. Corruption in the saints, is like sap in the green wood, which resisteth the fire, and will not burn well, till it be dried up. Prepared Paul had an heart mortified in a very high degree, to all the honour and riches of the world, accounting them all but trifles, Gal. 6:14, 1 Cor. 4:3, 4.

The need of this will be evinced by these five considerations.

1. Unless the heart be mortified to all earthly enjoyments, they will appear great and glorious things in your eye and estimation; and if so, judge what a task you will have, to deny and leave them all in a suffering hour. It is corruption *within*, that puts the lustre and glory upon things *without*: it is the carnal eye only that gazes admiringly after them, 2 Cor. 5:16, and hence the *lust* is put to express the *affection*, 1 John 2:16, because all that inordinate affection we have to them, arises from our high estimation of them, and that estimation from our lusts, that represent them as great and glorious. Therefore, certainly, it will be difficult (if not impossible) to deny them, till they have lost their glory in your eye; and that they will never do, till those lusts within you, that put that beauty and necessity upon them, be first crucified. As for instance, what a glory and necessity doth the pride of men put upon the honour and credit of the world, so that they will rather choose to die, than survive it? But to a mortified soul it is a *small matter*, 1 Cor. 4:3. So for riches, how much are they adored, till our lusts be mortified? and then they are esteemed but *dung and dross*, Phil. 3:8. It is our corruptions that paint and gild over these things; when these are crucified, those will be lightly esteemed.

2. Mortification of corruptions is that which recovers an healthful state of soul: sin is to the soul, what a disease is to the body; and mortification is to sin, what physic is to a disease. Hence those that are but a little mortified, are in a comparative sense called *carnal*, 1 Cor. 3:3, and *babes*, verse 1, in respect of weakness. Now, suffering work being some of the Christian's hardest labour and exercise, he cannot be fitted for it, until his soul be in an healthful state: a sickly

man cannot carry heavy burdens, or endure hard labours and exercises: the sick soldier is left behind in his quarters, or put into the hospital, whilst his fellows are dividing the spoils, and obtaining glorious victories in the field. To this sense some expound Rom. 8:13. 'If ye live after the flesh, ye shall die; but if ye through the Spirit, do mortify the deeds of the body, ye shall live.' Whereas *death* is put to note a languishing state of soul, whilst mortification is neglected; so *life* is put to express an healthful and comfortable state; *vivere pro valere*;[1] so that upon this account also the necessity of it appears.

3. Your *corruptions* must be mortified, else they will be raging and violent in the time of temptation, and, like a torrent, sweep away all your convictions and resolutions. It is sin unmortified within that makes the heart like gunpowder; so that when the sparks of temptation fly about it (and they fall thick in a suffering hour), they do but touch and take. Hence the *corruptions of the world* are said to be *through lust*, 2 Pet. 1:4. With these internal unmortified lusts the *tempter* holds correspondence; and these be the *traitors* that deliver up our souls into his hands.

4. Unless you be diligent and successful in this work, though you should suffer; yet not like Christians; you will but disgrace religion, and the cause for which you suffer; for it is not simple suffering, but suffering *as a Christian*, that reflects credit on religion, and finds acceptation with God. If you be envious, fretful, discontented, and revengeful, under your sufferings, what honour will this bring to Christ? Is not this altogether unlike the example of your Lord? Isa. 53:7, and the behaviour of suffering saints? 1 Cor.

---

[1] 'To live' is used instead of 'to live healthily'.

4:13. Yet thus it will be, if your pride, passion, and revenge, be not first subdued: for what are the breakings forth of such distempers of spirit, but as the flushes of heat in the face from an ill-affected liver? Most certain it is, that all the evils are in your natures, and as certain it is, they will rise like mud and filth from the bottom of a lake, when some eminent trials shall rake you to the bottom; *Natura vexata prodit seipsam.*[1]

5. Lastly, Mortification must be studied and plied with diligence; else you will find many longings and hankerings after earthly enjoyments and comforts, which will prove a snare to you: what is sin but the *corrupt* and *vitiated appetite* of the *creature*, to things that are earthly and sensual, relishing more sweetness and delight in them, than in the blessed God? And what is sanctification, but the rectifying of these *inordinate affections*, and placing them on their proper object? A regenerate and mortified Christian tastes not half that sweetness in forbidden fruits that another doth: set but money before Judas, and see how eagerly he catches at it – 'What will ye give me, and I will betray him?' Set but life, liberty, or any such bait before an unmortified heart, and how impotent is he to withstand them, as offered in a temptation? Oh those unmortified lusts! how do they make men hanker, long, and their lips water (as we use to say) after these things? This makes them break prison, decline sufferings, though upon the basest terms; whereas a mortified Christian can see all these things set before him, yea, offered to him, and refuse them, Heb. 10:35. It is with them much as it was with old Barzillai, 2 Sam. 19:35. When nature is decayed, they find but little pleasure in natural

[1] 'When nature is troubled, it reveals its true character.'

actions, Eccles. 12:1. And look as the body of sin decays and languishes, so do these longings also: It weans the soul from them all, and enables it to live very comfortably without them, Psa. 131:1, Phil. 4:12. There needs no more to be said to evince the necessity of mortification, and discover what influence it hath into a Christian's readiness for sufferings.

It remains therefore, that I open to you some of the principal *corruptions*, about which it mostly concerns you to bestow pains ere sufferings come. Now look as there are four principal enjoyments, in which you are like to be tried, viz. *Estate, name, liberty, life*; so the Christian work in suffering times lies in mortifying these four special *corruptions*, viz. *First*, The love of the world. *Secondly*, Ambition. *Thirdly*, Inordinate affection of freedom and pleasure. *Fourthly*, Excessive love of life.

1. For the love of this world, away with it, crucify it, crucify it: down with the idol, and let it be dethroned in all that intend to abide with Christ in the hour of temptation: how else will you take the spoiling of your goods? How will you be able to part with all for Christ, as these blessed souls did? It grieves my heart to see how many professors of religion are carried captive at the chariot wheels of a bewitching world. Oh! good had it been for many professors if they had never tasted so much of the sweetness of it. Sirs, I beg you for the Lord's sake, down with it in your *estimations*, down with it in your *affections*, else temptations will down with you ere long. I shall offer five or six helps for the crucifying of it.

First, Consider your espousals to Christ, and how you have chosen and professed him for your Lord and husband:

therefore your doting upon the world is no less than adultery against Christ, James 4:4. If Christ be your husband, he must be a covering to your *eyes*; an unchaste glance upon the world wounds him.

Secondly, The more you prize it, the more you will be tormented by it; did you prize and love it less, it would disquiet and vex you less: it is our doting on it that makes it draw blood at parting.

Thirdly, Get true scripture-notions of the world, and rectify your judgments and affections by them. If you will have the *true picture* and *representation* of it drawn by the hand of God himself, see 1 John 2:16, it is nothing else but a *phantastic glory*, and that also passeth away. What is become of them that ruffled it out in the world but one hundred years ago?[1] What could the world do for them? Are they not all gone down to the sides of the pit? 'But he that doth the will of God abideth for ever.'

Fourthly, Study and contemplate Christ and the things above more: this would veil all its glory, and kill it at the root, Phil. 3:18, 19. Just as a man that hath been gazing upon the sun, when he takes off his eye from that bright and glorious *creature*, and looks to the earth, there is a veil of darkness overspreading the face of it, that he can see nothing. I wonder how such as pretend to live above, and enjoy communion with God, can ever relish such sweetness in the world, or have their hearts enticed and captivated by it.

Fifthly, Remember always, that by your love and delight in worldly things, you furnish the devil with the chiefest bait he hath to catch and destroy your souls. Alas! were your

---

[1] A reference to the many martyrs of the English Reformation.

hearts but dead to these things, he would want an handle to catch hold on. What hath he more to offer you, and tempt you off from Christ with but a little money, or some such poor temporal rewards? and how little would that soul be moved by such a temptation, that looks on it all but as dirt?

Sixthly, Lastly, Take notice of the approaches of *eternity*: remember you are almost at the end of time: and when you come to launch out into that endless ocean, how will these things look then? It seems glorious whilst you are in the chase and pursuit of it: but upon a deathbed you will overtake and come up with it, and then you will see what a deceitful and vain thing it is: stand by the beds of dying men, and hear how they speak of it. O! the difference betwixt our apprehensions then and now! Thus labour to wean off your affections, and crucify them to the world.

2. Mortify your *ambition* and vain *affectation* of the repute and credit of the world: Oh stand not on so vain a thing as this: judge it but a small thing to be judged of man, to have your names cast out as evil: let not *scoffs* and *reproaches* be such terrible things to you. It is, without doubt, a great trial; else the Holy Ghost had not added a peculiar *epithet* to it, which is not given to any other of the sufferings of the saints: not cruel tortures, nor cruel stonings, burnings, slaying with the sword; but *cruel mockings*, Heb. 11:36. Yet learn to be dead to, and unaffected with these things; set the reproaching world as light and as low as it sets you: *Despise the shame*, as your master Christ did, Heb. 12:2. And to promote *mortification* in this, take these helps.

First, Consider this is no new or strange thing that hath happened to you: the holiest of men have passed through the like, if not worse trials, Heb. 10:33, Psa. 44:14. Reproaches have been the lot of the best men. They called Athanasius, Sathanasius; Cyprianus, Coprianus, a gatherer of dung; blessed Paul, *a pestilent fellow*; Dr Story threw a faggot at sweet Mr Denlie's face as he was singing a psalm in the midst of the flames, saying, *I have spoiled a good old song*.

Secondly, It may be religion hath been reproached and scoffed at for your sakes; and if so, think it not much to be reproached for religion's sake.

Thirdly, It is much better to be reproached by men for discharging duty than by your own consciences for the neglect of it; if all be quiet within, never be moved at the noise and clamour without: If you have a good roof over your head, be not troubled though the winds and storms bluster abroad, 1 Pet. 4:14. Take heed what you do, and be heedless what the world says.

Fourthly, Always remember, that you neither stand nor fall at the world's judgment, and therefore have the less reason to be troubled at it, 1 Cor. 4:3. If your condition were to be cast to eternity by it, it were somewhat.

Fifthly, There is a worth and excellency in the reproaches of Christ, as bad as they seem; and such an excellency, as it is not to be matched by any earthly enjoyment, Heb. 11:26. The reproaches of Christ are of more worth than the treasures of Egypt, though Egypt then was the magazine of the world for treasures. The apostles counted them their honours, Acts 5:41. When Ludovicus Marsacus, a knight of France, saw those that were to suffer with him in the chains, and that they put none upon him, because of the nobility of his birth, he said to the executioner, *Cur me non quoque*

torqui donast et illustris illius ordinis militem non creas?
'Why do ye not honour me with a chain too, and create me
a knight of that noble order?'

Sixthly, Lastly, Should scoffs and reproaches scare you
from Christ and duty; then, though you should escape the
reproaches of men, yet shall you fall under the everlasting
contempt of God, angels, and good men. Therefore, 'Fear
ye not the reproaches of men that shall die, nor be afraid
of their revilings, for the moth shall eat them up like a
garment, and the worm shall eat them like wool, but my
righteousness shall be for ever, and my salvation from
generation to generation,' Isa. 51:7, 8.

3. Mortify your *inordinate affections* of liberty, pleasure,
and delicate living. O let not a prison seem so formidable to
you. It is true, as Christ told Peter, in John 21:18, 'When thou
wast young, thou girdest thyself, and walkedst whither thou
wouldest; but when thou shalt be old, thou shalt stretch
forth thine hands, and another shall gird thee, and carry
thee whither thou wouldest not.' You have now your liberty
to go whither you will, and it is a precious mercy if well
improved; the birds of the air (as one saith) had rather be
in the woods at liberty, though lean and hungry, than in a
golden cage with the richest fare. But yet, if God will call
you to deny this also for Christ, see that you be ready to
be bound as Paul was, and receive the chain and bonds of
Christ with thanksgiving: To which end consider,

Firstly, That the affliction, in such cases of restraint, is
more from within, than from without you. There is no place
but may be delectable to you, if your heart be heavenly, and
the presence of God be engaged with you. What a sweet

night had Jacob at Bethel! Paul and Silas in the stocks! See that precious *letter* of Pomponius Algerius.

> *Transtulit in coelum Christi praesentia claustrum;*
> *Quid faciet coelo quae coelum jam creat antro?*[1]

It is your own unbelief and impatiency that gives you more trouble than the condition.

Secondly, No *keeper* can keep the Comforter from you, if you be the *Lord's prisoners*, Acts 16. If they could bar out the Spirit from you, it would be a dismal place indeed: But ordinarily, there the saints have their clearest *visions* of God, and sweetest *presence* of the Spirit. You are the Lord's *freemen*, whilst men's *prisoners*: All the world cannot divest you of the *state of liberty* Christ hath purchased for you, John 8:36.

Thirdly, Though a *prison* looks sad and dismal, yet it is not *hell*: Oh bless God for that, that is a sad prison indeed! Beloved, men have their *prisons*, and God hath his: *God's prison is a terrible prison*, indeed, thousands are now there in chains, 1 Pet. 3:19, and there you deserved to have been sent long ago: If God exchange an *hell* for a *prison*, have you any cause to complain?

Fourthly, How obdurate and cruel soever men are to you, yet the *Lord Jesus* is kind and tender-hearted to his *prisoners*; he puts the kindnesses that any shew them upon his own account, Matt. 25:36. 'He looks down from heaven to hear the sighings and groanings of his prisoners,' Psa. 102:20. He will tenderly sympathize with you in all your *prison-straits* and *troubles*.

[1]   If the presence of Christ once changed a prison into a kind of heaven,
What will it do in heaven itself, which even here doth make a dungeon like heaven?

Fifthly, A *prison* hath been handselled and perfumed by the best and holiest of men in all ages, 1 Kings 22:27, Jer. 32:2, Matt. 4:12, Acts 5:18 and 26:10. God hath made it a settled *school of discipline* to them.

Sixthly, Should, you, to avoid a *prison*, commit a sin, instead of being man's *prisoner*, you shall be clapped up by God, for he hath a prison for your souls even in this world, Psa. 142:7. And this is ten thousand times more dreadful than any *dungeon* in the world. Oh it is a *dark prison*! nothing to let in the least *beam of God's countenance* upon your poor *souls*. What a sad exchange have you made then?

Seventhly, Consider what a ground of comfort God hath laid in that word, Rev. 2:10, to obviate the fears and terrors incident to us in such a condition: God hath limited Satan and his instruments, both for time, number, and all circumstances of the trial.

Eighthly, Lastly, You do not know what a mercy may be in it: It may be a time of retirement from the world, and the clamours and distractions that are abroad. These days of imprisonment may be your holy days; as a prisoner of Christ once called them.

4. Get an heart mortified to the excessive and inordinate love of life: This, I confess, is the highest and hardest point of *self-denial*, because it wraps up all other *self-interests* in it. But yet consider.

First, Though life be very dear, yet Jesus Christ is ten thousand times dearer than thy life: If you be a saint he is the life of thy life, and the length of thy days; and in comparison of him and his glory, saints should, and have despised and slighted their lives, Luke 14:26, Rev. 12:11.

Secondly, Die you must: and if by shrinking from Christ you should protract a miserable life for a few days longer, in the meantime losing that *which is better than life*, Psa. 63:3, Matt. 10:39. Oh! when you lie upon your deathbed, you will wish that you had obeyed God's call, and so have departed in peace.

Thirdly, If you have cordially covenanted with Christ (as all sincere believers have done), then you have yielded up your lives to him, to be disposed of for his glory, Rom. 14:7. So that, look as Christ both lived and died for you; so *ought you to live as Christ*: And all the excellency you see in life consists in that reference and subserviency it hath to his glory. I say then, if you have understandingly and cordially transacted in a covenant way with him, your care will not be so much how to shun death, as by what death you may most glorify God, John 21:19. And certainly you can never lay them down upon a more honourable and comfortable account than in his cause, and for his sake. It was a great trouble to Luther, that he carried his blood to his grave.

Fourthly, To die for Christ, is one of the highest testifications of your love to Christ, that you are capable of, John 13:37. Yea, it is such a testification of your love to the Lord Jesus, as angels are not capable of making.

Fifthly, Why should you decline even a violent death for Christ, when as the bitterness of death is past, and there is no *hell* following the *pale horse*? It cannot separate you from Christ, Rom. 8:38.

Sixthly, Think what a death Christ suffered for you: In which the fulness of the wrath both of God and man met together, so that he was sore amazed; yet with desire did he desire it for your sakes.

Lastly, Think what a life you shall have with Christ as soon as this is delivered up to, and for him, 2 Tim. 2:12. It is but wink, and you shall see God.

Oh that these things might provoke you to follow on, and ply the work of *mortification*.

Chapter 11

Wherein is opened the singular advantage that suffering saints have by their skill and insights into the rewards and mysteries of Satan's temptations: some of those wiles of Satan opened, and rules for the avoiding of the danger briefly prescribed.

THE hazards and dangers of Christians in times of persecution, arise not so much from their sufferings, as from the temptations that always attend, and are by Satan planted upon their sufferings: for the most part, sufferings and temptations go together, Heb. 11:37. And therefore it behoves such as are, or expect to be called to sufferings, to dive into the mysteries of temptations, and be well acquainted with the enemy's designs upon them. So was Paul, and so he supposes all others to be that engage in the same cause: 'We are not ignorant of his devices,' 2 Cor. 2:11. There is a manifold advantage redounding to suffering saints thereby.

1. He that is well acquainted with the methods of temptation, will be better able to descry the first approaches and beginnings of it, and a temptation discovered, is more than half conquered. It is a special artifice of Satan to shuffle in his temptations as indiscernibly as may be into the soul; for he knows, that 'in vain is the net spread in the sight of any bird,' Prov. 1:17. And therefore he ordinarily makes a suffering season to be a tempting season; because sufferings,

like fire to iron, make it impressive and operable, they do ordinarily put the soul into an hurry and distraction, and so gives him an advantage to tempt the soul with less suspicion and greater success. But now, a skilful Christian that is acquainted with his wiles, will discern when he begins to *enter into temptation*; as Christ's expression is, Luke 22:46. And so check the temptation in its first rise when it is weakest, and most easily broken. Doubtless one reason why so many fall by temptation is, because it is got within them, and hath prevailed far before it be discovered to be a temptation.

2. He that is well acquainted with Satan's methods of tempting, will not only discern it sooner than another; but also knows his work and duty, and how to manage the conflict with it, which is a great matter. There are many poor souls that labour under strong temptations, and know not what to do: They go up and down complaining from Christian to Christian, whilst the judicious Christian plies to the *throne of grace* with strong cries, see 2 Cor. 12:8, keeps up his watch, Luke 22:46, countermines the temptation, by assaulting that *corruption*, by endeavours of *mortification*, which Satan assaults by temptation, 1 Cor. 9:27.

3. Lastly, To name no more; he that is best acquainted with the *mystery of temptation*, and can maintain his ground against it, he shall be the preserving Christian under persecutions, and the victorious Christian over them. Here lies the main design of Satan, in raising persecution against the saints. It is not so much their blood that he thirsteth after, as their fall by temptation: and all persecutions are designed by him to introduce his temptations. These work upon our fear, and fear drives us into his trains and snares,

Prov. 29:25. The devil's work in raising persecution, is but as the fowler's work in beating the bush in the night, when the net is spread to take the birds, which he can affright out of their coverts. He that understands that, is not easily moved by the strongest opposition, from his place and duty; and so is like to prove the most constant and invincible Christian in times of persecution.

Oh! then, how necessary is it, that since all persecutions are intended as means to promote temptation, and that skill and insight into these designs of Satan so advantages as to frustrate his designs in both? I say, how necessary is it that you should be all instructed wherein the strength of temptation lies; as also how to resist those strong and dangerous temptations, which your sufferings only are intended to usher in, and make way for?

It will not be unseasonable or impertinent, then, in this chapter, to shew you, *First*, Wherein the force and efficacy of temptation lieth; *Secondly*, What you are to do, when in a suffering hour such temptation shall assault you. And,

First, Question: Wherein doth the efficacy and power of temptation lie?

Solution: I answer, It lies principally in three things.

1. In the kind and nature of the temptation.

2. In the craft and policy of Satan in managing it.

3. In that secret correspondency that Satan hath with our corruptions.

1. It lies in the kind and nature of the temptation itself; for it is most certain, that all temptations are not alike forcible and dangerous. Some are ordinarily more successful than others; and such are these that follow.

(i.) Strange and unusual temptations, I mean not such as none have been troubled with before us; for there is not a dart in Satan's quiver, but hath been let fly at the breasts of other saints, before it was levelled at ours, 1 Cor. 10:13. But by strange and unusual, I mean such as the people of God are but rarely troubled with, and possibly we were never exercised with before. These are the more dangerous, because they daunt and amaze the soul, and ordinarily beget despondency, even as some strange disease would do that we know not what to make of, nor can learn that others have been sick of.

(ii.) Mark them for most dangerous temptations, that are *adapted* and suited to your proper sin, or *evil constitution*: For certainly that is the most dangerous crisis of temptation when it tries a man there. Now, if he be not truly gracious, he falls by the root irrecoverably, Luke 22:5, 6. Or if sincere, yet without special assistance, and extraordinary vigilance, he falls scandalously, 2 Sam. 11:2 compared with 1 Sam. 16:12.

(iii.) When it is a *spiritual temptation*, which rises indiscernibly out of the Christian's duties. This is the less suspected, because temptations usually come from the strength and liveliness of *corruptions*; but this, from the slaughter and conquests we make of them. Duties and enlargements in them, which are the poison of other lusts, prove the food and fuel of this, 1 Cor. 4:7, 8. And how much the more covert and close any temptation is, by so much the more dangerous it is.

2. The strength and efficacy of temptation lies much in the skill and policy of Satan in the management of it: And hence they are called wiles, methods and devices, 2 Cor. 2:11, Eph. 6:11, and himself an old serpent, Rev. 12:9. And

among the rest of his deep and desperate stratagems these following are remarkable,

(i.) In employing such instruments to manage his temptations as are least suspected, and have the greatest influence. *A teacher*, Gal. 2:14. *A wife*, Gen 3:6, Job 2:9. *Friends*, Acts 21:13. The devil knows it is a bad business, and therefore must make the best of it; Paul's sorest trial was by his dearest friends.

(ii.) In the orderly disposition and ranging of his temptations, beginning with little things first, and then by degrees working over to greater. His first motions are commonly most modest, Gen. 3:1. Should he discover the depth of his design at first, it would startle the soul, and make it reply as Hazael, 'Am I a dog that I should do thus?' It is far easier to gain his end by parts, than putting for all at once.

(iii.) In endeavouring to engage the soul upon his own ground. I mean to tempt him from his station and duty where God sets, and expects to find him. He knows while you are with God, God is with you, 2 Chron. 15:2. Whilst a man abides there, he abides with God, 1 Cor. 7:24. Whilst he is there, the promise is a good breastwork to keep off all his darts: And therefore, as fishers, when they have spread their nets in the river, beat the fishes out of their coverts and caverns; so doth Satan.

(iv.) In not presenting the temptation, till the soul be prepared to receive it. He loves to strike when the iron is hot. He first lets their troubles come to an height, brings them to the prison, gibbet, or fire, and then offers them deliverance, Heb. 11:35, 37.

(v.) In tiring our souls with a long continuance of temptations. What he cannot win by a *sudden storm* he hopes to gain by a *tedious siege*. Forty days together he assaulted the Captain of our salvation, Mark 1:13. And truly it is a wonder the soul yields not at last, that hath been tried long, Psa. 125:3, 'When the rod of the wicked lies long upon the back of the righteous, it is much if he put not forth his hand to iniquity.'

(vi.) In falling most violently upon them, when they are lowest and most prostrate in their spirits and comforts: So he assaulted Job with a temptation, *to curse God and die*, when he sat in that deplorable state upon the dunghill, Job 2:8, 9. He loves to fall upon us, as Simeon and Levi did upon the Shechemites, when we are sore and wounded: And therefore ordinarily you find times of *divine desertions* to be times of *diabolical temptations*. So that, look, as the wild beasts of the desert come out of their dens in the night, and then roar after their prey, Psa. 104:20, so doth Satan, when the soul seems to be benighted and lost in the darkness of spiritual troubles.

And this is the second thing wherein the efficacy and strength of temptation lies.

3. Lastly, It lies in that secret correspondency Satan holds with our bosom enemies. Were it not for this *domestic traitor*, he could not surprise us so easily: As you see in Christ; he could do nothing because he found nothing to fasten a temptation on. He was like a *crystal glass* filled with pure fountain water: So that though he should have been agitated and shaken never so much by temptation, yet no filthy sediment could appear; but now we have an enemy within that holds intelligence with Satan without; and this would prove a *devil* to us, if there were no other *devil* to tempt us, James 1:14, 15. It is a fountain of temptation in

itself, Matt. 15:19, and the chief instrument by which Satan doth all his tempting work, 2 Pet. 1:4.

Our several passions and affections are the handles of his temptations. Everything, saith Epictetus, hath δυο λαβας [*duo labas*], two handles to take it by. Our affections are the handles of our souls. The temptation of self-confidence and pride takes hold of a daring and forward disposition, the temptation of apostasy upon a timorous disposition, etc. These inbred lusts go over to the enemy in the day of battle, and fight against the soul, 1 Pet. 2:11. This is a more dangerous enemy than the *devil*. It is true they both work against us, but with a double difference. Satan works *externally* and *objectively*; but lust *internally* and *physically*, i.e. *quoad materale*, as it is capable of physical efficiency. 'Sin wrought in me all manner of concupiscence,' Rom. 8:8. Yea, it is a subtle enemy that doth his business politicly, Rom. 7:11, *Sin deceived me*; it betrays with a kiss, strangles with a *silken halter*, Heb. 12:1, Eph. 4:22. These be his agents sitting at the *council table* in our own breasts, and there carrying on his designs effectually: Yea, it is the restless and perpetual enemy, no ridding your hands of him. Satan is sometimes put to flight by resistance, James 4:7, and sometimes ceases his temptations, Luke 4:13. But when he ceaseth to *tempt* and *inject*, this ceaseth not to irritate and solicit; where we are, it will be; it is our sad lot to be tied to it, and perpetually assaulted by it, Rom. 7:24. We may say of it as Hannibal said of Marcellus, that it is never quiet, whether a *conqueror*, or conquered; yea, it is a potent enemy too, it hauls men away to the commission of sin, James 1:14, it seizeth the magazine of the soul, and delivers up the arms, I mean the members, to be ὅπλα ἀδικίας [*hopla adikias*], weapons of unrighteousness.

Thus you see wherein the efficacy and power of temptation consists. And it mightily concerns you that are, or expect to be sufferers for Christ, to be acquainted with these things, and know where the strength of your enemy lies.

But how shall the suffering saint so manage himself in a suffering hour, as not to be captivated by temptations? This brings me upon the *second* thing I promised; viz. to prescribe some rules for the escaping or conquering of those temptations that are incidental to a suffering state. And first,

Rule 1. Labour to cut off the advantages of temptations before they come. It is our inordinate love to life, estate, liberty, and ease, that gives the temptations so much strength upon us. Do not overvalue them, and you will more easily part from them, Rev. 12:11. O mortify self-love, and creature-love; let your heart be loosened and weaned from them, and then the temptation hath lost its strength.

Rule 2. Secure to yourselves an interest in the heavenly glory. When once you clearly see your propriety in the kingdom above, you will set the lighter and lower by all things on earth. That is a pregnant text to this purpose, Heb. 10:34. It is our darkness and uncertainties about those that make us cling so fast to these.

Rule 3. Settle this principle in your heart as that which you will never depart from, that it is better for you to fall into any suffering, than into the least sin, Heb. 11:24, 25. This all will acknowledge, but how few practise it! Oh that you would practically understand and receive it! Suffering is but a *respective*, *external*, and *temporal* evil; but sin is an universal, internal, and everlasting evil.

Rule 4. Believe that God hath cursed and blasted all the ways of sin, that they shall never be a shelter to any soul that flies for refuge to them, Mark 8:35, Prov. 13:15. The way of transgressors is a hard and difficult way. There is no security in the way of iniquity. He that runs from suffering to sin, runs from the seeming to the real danger; from the painted to the living lion.

Rule 5. Live up to this principle that there is no policy like sincerity and godly simplicity. This will preserve and secure you when carnal wisdom will expose and betray you. Psa. 25:2, Job 2:3. Sinful policy never thrives with saints.

Rule 6. Consider sadly what the consequence of yielding up yourselves to temptations will be: The name of God will be dreadfully reproached, 2 Sam. 12:14. A fatal stumbling-block is laid before the blind world, 1 Sam. 2:36. The hearts of many upright ones made sad, Psa. 25:3. The fall of a professor is as when a standard-bearer fainteth; and a dreadful wound it will be to thine own conscience, 2 Cor. 2:7, Matt. 25:46. One hour's sleep of security may keep you many days and nights waking upon the rack of horror.

Rule 7. Never engage a temptation in your own strength, but go forth against it trembling in yourselves, and relying on divine aids and assistances, Eph. 6:10. What! are you to grapple with spirits, to enter the lists with *principalities* and *powers*? Or what is your strength that you should hope?

Rule 8. Let the days of your temptation be days of strong cries and supplications. Thus did Paul, 2 Cor. 12:8, Psa. 109:4. Your best posture to wrestle with temptation, is upon your knees.

Rule 9. Dwell upon the consideration of those choice encouragements God hath laid up in the world for such a

PREPARATIONS FOR SUFFERINGS

time. As, (1.) Though he give Satan leave to tempt you, yet you are still in his hand to preserve you, Deut. 33:3, John 10:28. (2.) That whilst Satan is sifting and trying you on earth, Christ is interceding for you in heaven, Luke 22:31, 32. (3.) That an eternal reward is laid up for those that overcome, Luke 22:28, 29, Rev. 21:7, 8. And now is this reward to be won or lost.

Rule 10. Lastly, Be content, till God open a door out of your temptations, 1 Cor. 10:13. The time of the promise will come, Acts 7:17. Wait for it, though it tarry, and seem to be deferred; in the end it will speak, and not lie, Hab. 2:3. There was a secret door in the ark, though it could not be seen whilst the waters prevailed: And so there is in all your temptations, though at present it be not discernible by you. And thus have I brought you one step nearer to Paul's blessed frame. O give diligence to make yourselves ready for sufferings.

Chapter 12

Sheweth that a choice part of our preparation and readiness for sufferings consists in the improvement of our praying abilities, and keeping close with God in that heavenly and excellent duty in days of suffering; wherein also is opened the nature and means of its improvement.

PRAYER is said to be amongst duties, as faith is amongst the graces. Doubtless it is of special use and service at all times to a Christian: But yet in suffering days it is of more than ordinary use and necessity, Heb. 4:16, James 5:13. And therefore it is reckoned among those choice pieces of armour which suffering saints are to put on, Eph. 6:18. I will here briefly discover the necessity of it, and then shew you that a Christian may improve himself to an excellent degree in it; and, lastly, prescribe some means for an improvement.

The necessity of it to a suffering saint will demonstratively appear, if you consider,

1. That this duty is the outlet of troubles, and the best way the poor Christian hath to ease his heart when surcharged with sorrow. Griefs are eased by groans. Such evaporations disburden and cool the heart, as the opening of a vein in some cases doth. Oh the sensible ease that comes in this way! When grief in the mind, like vapours in the air, are condensed into black clouds that overspread the soul, and

darken that beautiful light that once shone there, then prayer, like the sun dispels and scatters them, 1 Sam. 1:18. Many a saint, by prayer, hath sucked the breast of a promise, and then fell asleep by divine contentment in the bosom of God. A time may come when thy heart is ready to break with trouble, and not a friend to whom thou canst open and ease it, and then blessed be God for prayer, Micah 7:5-7. That which sinks others is, that when troubles fill and over-whelm their hearts, they try what reason, merry company, or outward comforts can do: But, alas! this is to palliate a cure, it returns again with the more violence: But prayer gives sensible relief, Psa. 102 *title*, Psa. 62:8. For, (i.) This opens and gives a vent to troubles, Jer. 20:12. (ii.) It gives our troubles a diversion, and so a cure, Psa. 5:1 and the last verse compared. Yea, (iii.) By praying over them they are not only diverted, but sanctified, and so cease to be distracting, or destroying troubles.

2. As it gives a vent to our troubles, so an inlet to unspeakable comforts and consolations. See a pregnant instance of this, Acts 16:25. For, (1.) Hereby they obtain gracious answers from the Lord concerning their troubles, 2 Cor. 12:9. In this also they meet the gracious smiles of God, which swallow up their troubles, Psa. 85:8. And, lastly, hereby they prevail with God to open a seasonable and effectual door out of all their troubles, Psa. 34:4, 6.

3. Prayer begets and maintains holy courage and magna-nimity in evil times. When all things about you tend to discouragement, it is your being with Jesus that makes you bold, Acts 4:13. He that is used to be before a great God, will not be afraid to look such little things as men are in the face. The woman clothed with the sun, had the moon under her

feet. And what need you have of courage in evil times, hath been already shewed.

4. This is a duty you may perform at any time, or in any condition: No adversary can cut you off from it. It cannot be said so of many other duties. None can hinder the intercourse betwixt heaven and your souls: You may perform it in a prison, Acts 16:25, in a banished condition, Psa. 61:2. And so is fitted for a suffering condition.

5. *Lastly*, You must strive to excel in this, forasmuch as no grace within, or service without, can thrive without it. God hath ordained the whole work of grace to grow up to perfection this way, Judg. 19:20. He will have all mercies fetched out this way, Ezek. 36:37, Jer. 29:11-13. All that comes from God to you, or to you from God, must come in this channel. Be convinced then of the need you have to improve yourselves herein, as ever you hope to stand in the evil day.

But how are these praying abilities capable of improvement in the people of God?

Praying abilities are either external and common, or else internal and special. The external and common ability is nothing else but that dexterity and skill men get to express themselves to God in prayer. Thus many can put their meaning into apt and decent expressions, to which the Spirit sometimes adds his common touches upon the affections. And this hypocrites rest on, and glory in. Or else they are special and internal, whereby men are enabled to pour out their souls to God in a gracious manner. And this may be considered either in the habit or the act. The habit is given by the Spirit, when the principles of grace are first infused into the soul, Zech. 12:10, Acts 9:11. By being sanctified we are made near, and by acting those principles in prayer we are said to draw near, Psa. 10:17. Now in our actual drawing near to God, the Spirit hath the chief and principal hand: And his assistance therein is threefold.

(1.) He excites the heart to the duty; it is he that whispers to the soul to draw nigh to God, Psa. 27:8.

(2.) He suggests the matter of our prayers, and furnishes us with the materials, Rom. 8:26, guiding us as to the matter, not only to what is lawful, but also to what is expedient for us.

(3.) He stirreth up suitable affections in prayer, Rom. 8:26. And hence those groans and tears, those gaspings and vehement anhelation.[1] But notwithstanding all our abilities, both habitual and actual, be from the Spirit, and not from ourselves, yet are they capable of improvement by us: For though in respect of acquirement, there be a great difference betwixt natural and supernatural habits, yet their improvement is in the same way and manner; and this improvement may be made divers ways: For,

First, Though you have the Spirit, and can pray, yet you may learn to pray more humbly than before: Though you rise no higher as to words, yet you may learn to lay yourselves lower before the Lord, as Abraham and Ezra did, Gen 18:27, Ezra 9:6.

Secondly, You may learn to pray with more sincerity than formerly: Ah! there is much *hypocrisy* and *formality* in our *prayers*, much of custom, etc. Now you may learn to pour out more *cordial prayers*. See Psa. 17:1, Psa. 119:10.

Thirdly, You may learn to pray with more zeal and earnestness than before: Some saints have excelled and been remarkable for this, Dan. 9:19, Hosea 12:4, James 5:16.

[1] Panting or shortness of breath.

Fourthly, With more assiduity and readiness at all times for it, Eph. 6:18. *Praying always*, with all prayer. Hence Christ gives that commendation to the church, Song of Sol. 4:11, 'Thy lips, O my spouse, drop as the honeycomb.' The *honeycomb* often drops, but always hangs full of drops ready to fall.

Fifthly, You may learn to pray with more faith: Oh the qualms of unbelief that go over our hearts in a duty; faith is the soul of prayer, and according to the faith God finds in them, he accepts and values them.

Now in all these things you may improve yourselves abundantly.

1. By being more frequent in the duty, Job 22:21, 'Acquaint thyself with the Almighty'; in the Hebrew it is, *accustom thyself*: Those that have been excellent have also been abundant in it, Psa. 16:7.

2. By taking heed that you grieve not the Spirit, on whose influences and assistances you so entirely depend: Even as much as a ship doth upon the gales of wind for its motion.

3. By honouring the Spirit which enables you to pray, and that especially two ways: (i.) By dependence on him; go not forth in your own strength to the duty, trust not to your own promptness, or preparations. (ii.) By returning, and with thankfulness ascribing the praise of all to him; lie humble under all enlargements: say, *Not I, but grace*.

4. By searching your own hearts, and examining your necessities and wants, when you draw nigh to God; this will be a fountain of matter, and give you a deep resentment[1] of the worth of mercies prayed for.

---

[1] Resentment = grateful appreciation or acknowledgement.

5. Lastly, By looking more at the exercise of graces, and less at the discovery of parts; by labouring for impressions more, and pumping for expressions less. And thus I have briefly shewed you how to furnish yourselves with this needful qualification also.

Chapter 13

*Wherein is shewed the necessity of going out of ourselves,
even when our habitual and actual preparations are at
the greatest height; and depending as constantly and
entirely upon the Spirit, who is Lord of all gracious influences, as if we had done nothing: together with the means
of working the heart to such a frame.*

Thus you have seen your habitual and actual readiness for
sufferings, and blessed is the soul that gives diligence to
this work: But now lest all that I have said and you have
wrought, should be in vain; I must let you know, that all this
will not secure you, unless you can, by humility, faith, and
self-denial, go out of yourselves to Christ, and live upon him
daily for supply of grace, as much as if you had none of all
this furniture and provision for sufferings. I confess grace is
a very beautiful and lovely creature, and it is hard for a man
to look upon his own graces, and not dote upon them. But
yet know, that if you had all these excellent preparations
that have been mentioned, yea, and all angelical perfections
superadded, yet are you not complete without this dependence upon Christ, Col. 2:10. Whenever you go forth to suffer
for Christ, you should say at the head of all your excellent
graces, duties, and preparations, as Jehoshaphat did, when
at the head of a puissant and mighty army, 2 Chron. 20:12,
'O Lord, I have no might nor strength, but my eyes are unto

thee.' This is one thing in which Paul excelled, and was a special part of his readiness. See 1 Cor. 15:10. What a poor creature is the eminentest saint, left to himself in an hour of trial? the *hop*, the *ivy*, and the *woodbine*, are taught by nature to cling about stronger props and supporters: What they do by nature, we should do by grace.

The necessity and great advantage of this will appear upon divers considerations.

Consideration 1. The Christian's own imbecility[1] and insufficiency, even in the strength and height of all his acquirements and preparations; what are you, to grapple with such an adversary? Certainly you are no match for him that conquered Adam hand to hand in his state of integrity. It is not your inherent strength that enables you to stand, but what you receive and daily derive from Jesus Christ, John 15:5, 'Without me,' or never so little separated from me, 'ye can do nothing; all your sufficiency is of God,' 2 Cor. 3:5. Upon this very consideration it was, that the apostle exhorts the Ephesians 'to be strong in the Lord, and in the power of his might,' i.e. not to depend upon their own stock and furniture; but divine assistances and daily communications; 'For we wrestle not with flesh and blood, but principalities and powers,' Eph. 6:10, 12. In his own strength shall no man prevail.

Consideration 2. It is the great design of God in the gospel to exalt his Son, and to have all glory attributed and ascribed to him, 'That in all things he might have the pre-eminence,' Col. 1:18. That Christ 'might be all, in all,' Col. 3:11. Hence no saint must have a self-sufficiency, or be

---

[1] Imbecility = weakness, feebleness, impotence.

trusted with a stock as Adam was, but Christ being filled with all the fulness of God, and made the πρωτον δεκτικον [*proton dektikon*], or first receptacle of all grace; 'For it pleased the Father, that in him all fulness should dwell'; all the saints are therefore to go to him for supplies, and of his fulness to receive, John 1:16. This fulness being a *ministerial fulness*, like that of the sun, or of a fountain, intended to supply all our wants. And hence it is that faith, a self-emptying and denying grace, is appointed to be the instrument of fetching our supplies from Christ. All must be derived from him, that all the praise and glory may be ascribed to him, Phil. 4:14. And this is a most wise and congruous ordination of God, for hereby not only are his people the better secured, but by this also the reproach that lay upon Christ is rolled away. He was reproached on earth, as barren, empty, weak; 'Can any good come out of Nazareth?' He was looked upon as a 'Root springing out of a dry ground,' but by this shall his reproach be wiped away: So that unless you will go about to cross the great design of God, in the exaltation of his Christ, you must go out of yourselves, and humbly and constantly rely upon supplies from Christ and his grace to help in the times of need.

Consideration 3. A Christian is constantly to depend upon Christ, notwithstanding all his own preparations and inherent qualifications: because the activity even of inherent grace depends upon him. Inherent grace is beholden to exciting and assisting grace for all it is enabled to do. You cannot act a grace without his Spirit, 1 Cor. 15:10, 2 Cor. 3:5, John 15:5. It may be said of grace in us, as it was of the land of Canaan, Deut. 11:10-12, 'It is not as the land of Egypt, whence ye came out, where thou sowedst thy seed, and wateredst it with thy foot, as a garden of herbs: but a land of hills and valleys, drinking water of the rain of heaven; a land which the Lord thy God careth for: his eyes are always upon it, from the beginning of the year even to the end of the year.' As the life and fragrancy of vegetables depend on the influences of heaven, so do our graces upon Christ. And hence he is called, (1.) A root, Isa. 11:10. (2.) An head, Col. 1:18. (3.) A sun, Mal. 4:2. (4.) A fountain, Zech. 13:1. All which comparisons do fully carry this truth in them.

Consideration 4. Lastly, In this life of dependence lies your security; and indeed this is the great difference betwixt the two *covenants*. In the first, Adam's stock was in his own hands, and so his security or misery depended upon the unconstrained choice of his own mutable and self-determining will. But now in the new covenant, all are to go to Christ, to depend upon him for supplies, and are so secured against all destructive dangers, Jude 1, 1 Pet. 1:5. Should you go forth in your own strength against a temptation, either your grace would fail, and you fall in the conflict; or if you obtain any victory over it by your own strength, yet it is a thousand to one but your pride would conquer you, when you had conquered it: Like him that slew an *elephant*, but was himself slain by the fall of that *elephant* which he slew. But now, by this way, as God hath secured you against the dangers without; so also the frame and constitution of this new covenant is such as prevents the danger arising from our own pride too. Not *Ego et Deus mens*: I and my God did this; as was once said by a profane mouth; 'but self is abased, and the Lord lifted up in his own strength,' 1 Cor. 5:7. And thus I have briefly evinced the necessity of this daily dependence.

But next it concerns you to know what this dependence we speak of is: this also I shall briefly open to you, laying down somewhat *negatively*, and somewhat *positively* about it.

1. *Negatively*. It is not to deny the grace wrought in us by the Spirit; this were both injustice and ingratitude; we may know our own graces so as to be thankful for them, though not so as to be proud of them, 1 Cor. 15:10.

2. *Negatively*. It is not a lazy excuse from our duty: you do not *depend*, but rather *dishonour* Christ, by so doing; you must not say, because Christ must do all, therefore I must do nothing: but rather work out your salvation, because it is he that worketh both to will and to do, Phil. 2:12, 13. These are not *opposed*, but *subordinated*.

But then positively, it lies in three things.

1. *Positively*. In seeing and acknowledging the infinite sufficiency on, and fulness that is in Christ: to acknowledge him to be all in all: not only by way of *impetration*[1] procuring all, Heb. 9:12, but also by way of *application*, bringing home to the soul all the blessings purchased by his blood, and settling us in the possession of it, John 14:3. And so from first to last to eye him as the author and finisher of our faith.

2. *Positively*. In seeing the necessary dependence that all our graces have upon him. So that as you see the stream depending on the fountain, the beam upon the sun, the branch upon the root, the building upon the foundation, even so do our graces upon Christ: on him they live, and cut off from him they die. 'Our life is hid with Christ in God,' Col. 3:3. When you see this, and also see that all your

---

[1] Impetration = the action of procuring by request or entreaty.

activity, and striving, is but as the hoisting up of the sails, in order to the motion of the ship, which can do nothing till there come a gale; when you look upon your grace as a creature that must be upheld, fed, acted, and preserved by Christ, Col. 2:19, then you are prepared for this act of dependence: As for instance, you can never depend upon Christ for the acting of that grace of hope, until you see Christ to be the prop and foundation of it, and that it depends upon him, as upon its cause, 1 Pet. 1:3, as upon its object, Heb. 6:19, and as upon its *foundation* and ground work, Col. 1:27.

You can never depend upon Christ for your joy and comfort, until you see what a necessary dependence this also hath upon him, Phil. 3:3, and that, both as to its being and acting, John 16:22.

You can never depend upon him, for strength in any duty, until you see how your duties depend upon Christ, not only for the *strength* by which they are performed, John 15:4, 5, but also for *acceptation* when they are performed, 1 Pet. 2:5. It were easy to instance in any other grace.

3. *Positively.* It lies in looking off from your own grace whenever you are put upon the acting of it (I mean in regard of any dependence upon it), and looking by an eye of faith for acceptation to Christ, Heb. 12:2.[1] To the putting forth of which act of dependence upon Christ, holy ejaculations in our own onsets upon duty, or those quick and vigorous liftings up of our souls to God that way, are of special use, it being a duty fitted for the purpose, when there is no room for set and solemn prayer. And thus briefly of its nature.

---

[1] ἀφορῶντες εἰς τὸν τῆς πίστεως ἀρχηγὸν [*aforontes eis ton teis pisteos archeigon*]. Looking off to the author of our faith.

And to urge you to this duty, I shall offer these seven considerations: which, oh, that they might prevail upon your hearts, and make you forever to clasp and cling about Christ more than ever you have done.

Consideration 1. You have little reason to rely upon the strength of your own graces, for you may be easily deceived in that matter, and think you have much more grace than you have. How often are the common gifts of the Spirit mistaken for his special graces! the sixth chapter to the Hebrews is able to make a man tremble in this thing.

Consideration 2. Suppose you have much grace, yet have you not strong corruptions, and may you not meet with strong temptations also? He that hath less of other graces than you, may have more humility and self-denial than you, and so may stand when you fall. Great enlargements are often attended with great temptations of pride, etc.

Consideration 3. Whatever measures of grace you have arrived at, yet all is not able to secure you from falling, if God withhold or withdraw his aids and influences. Abraham had more faith than you, and yet he fell into a sin contrary to that very grace wherein he so excelled others, Gen. 20:2. Job had more patience than you; which of you could behave yourselves as he did, had you been in the like circumstances as he was? chap. 1:1, he is renowned for it in the scripture, James 5:11, yet he fell into that sin which is contrary to this grace also, chap. 3. Moses had more *meekness* than you: 'Now the man Moses was the meekest man upon the earth.' If you be but reproved, and that justly for your faults, how waspish are you? Yet see how this grace failed even in him, in an eminent trial of it, Num. 9:13-15. Adam was much more advantaged in this respect than you, being made upright, and no corruption inherent in him, yet he fell; the *angels* more again, yet they fell. Oh when will you learn the vanity of self-dependence.

Consideration. 4. Nothing more provoketh the Lord to withdraw his Spirit, and let you fall, than this sin of self-confidence doth, Luke 14:19-21. God will teach you by sad experience your own weakness, and what frail and vain things you be, if you will learn it by no other means.

Consideration. 5. If God permit you to fall (as doubtless he will, if you be self-conceited), then the more eminent you have been, or are for grace, the more will the name of God be reproached by your fall. This will furnish the triumphs of the uncircumcised, and the lamentations of your brethren, and make them say, 'How are the mighty fallen!' What dismal consequents will attend your fall.

Consideration. 6. Have you not sad experience of your own weakness from day to day in your lesser trials? Have you not said in some smaller conflicts, as David once did, 'My feet had well nigh slipped.' O methinks this should teach you to look more to God, and less to self: 'If you have run with footmen, and they have wearied you in the land of peace, *think sadly how* you should contend with horses in the swellings of Jordan.' Do not you see that you are but feathers in the wind of temptation? Consult your former experiences, and they will tell you what weaklings you are.

Consideration. 7. Lastly, Hath Christ given you more grace than others, then how much more hath he obliged you to honour him thereby? And is this your requital of his love! What! to take the crown from his head, and put it upon your own! Certainly a greater injury cannot be done to Christ than this.

Well then, by all this be persuaded to cease from your-selves, yea, from your religious selves; and to all your other preparations, add this as a choice one; if you do these things; you shall never fall. And thus you see the complete Christian in his equipage for sufferings.

Chapter 14

Containing the first use of the point by way of conviction, discovering the unreadiness of multitudes of professors for suffering-work.

You have seen, by all that hath been spoken, what the necessary prerequisites unto a suffering condition are; and what manner of persons you must be (both for habitual and actual readiness), if ever you honour Christ by bonds, or death for him. And I doubt not but your judgments and consciences yield to the evident necessity of these things, wherein I have placed the Christian's readiness. But, alas! where shall we find among the throngs and crowds of professors, any considerable numbers thus qualified and prepared? To suffer for Christ is a gift that few have received. We are fallen into the dregs of time. O how little of primitive zeal and simplicity remains among the professors of this age! latter times have produced a sort of professors of another stamp and spirit. These have the *light*, but they had the *love*: these *see* more, but they *did* and *suffered* more. How many that are no ornament to religion, do adorn themselves with the name of it!

Now, according to this account given of a ready Christian, divers professing persons will be convicted of their unreadiness and stability to manage suffering-work: As first,

1. The politic and hypocritical professors, whose hearts were never *set right* at first, and therefore cannot be *steadfast* when trials come, Psa. 78:8. Their hearts were never *sound in God's statutes*, and therefore no wonder if they be not only a *shame to*, but *ashamed of* their profession, Psalm 119:80. Never wonder if you see that profession which began in *hypocrisy*, to end in *apostasy*. These want their habitual readiness for sufferings, and so cannot drink of that cup: Needs must they fall when tried; and when they fall, they fall dreadfully, and often irrecoverably; for they neither have the *seed of God in them*, nor any *promise* of God made to them.

And are there not many such to be found in every place? For, (1.) How difficult is it to persuade many of you to any duty that hath loss or hazard attending on it? Doth not the sincere heart stand inclinable and disposed to all the known will of God? Psalm 119:6. Do Christians use to enquire more what is cheap, easy, and safe for them, or what is their duty? Gal. 1:16. Speak conscience, for to thee do I appeal; art thou not conscious of some reserves, limitations, and exceptions? Doth not the man, like Naaman, desire the Lord to excuse and pardon him in this or that thing? 2 Kings 5:17. And thinkest thou that this is consistent with sincere obedience, which excepts no duty, nor quarrels with any command, because they all bow equally from the sovereignty of God, James 2:11, and so doth what it doth *intuitu voluntatis*, upon the sight of God's will. Say conscience, are there not great strugglings, disputes, and contests betwixt thee and fleshly interests in such cases? And art thou not frequently over-borne? O search your hearts in this particular.

(2.) Yea, *secondly*, I appeal to you, whether there be not many among you that choose sin rather than affliction?

This is always the hypocrite's option and choice: He judges sufferings the greatest evils, and so orders himself in his election. It was merely to avoid persecution that those hypocrites, Gal. 6:12, constrained others to be circumcised only to gratify the Jews; that so by a sinful compliance with them, the offence of the cross might cease. If Paul would have done so, he might have avoided it too, but he durst not whatever he suffered, Gal. 5:11. O this is a shrewd sign of a false heart, Job 36:21. And the contrary disposition is always found in the upright heart, Heb. 11:25.

Nay, are there not some that have, and others that are ready to throw up their professions, when they see into what difficulties it involves them? Whilst they could live upon the profession of truth, they entertained it; but when truth comes to live upon them, they thrust it out, and cry, away with this profession, it will beggar and undo us: They then repent of their forwardness, and secretly wish they had never engaged in it. O examine whether your hearts be not thus turned back, and your steps declined. If so, it is manifest you are hypocritical professors, and that it was some outward self-respect at first engaged you in your profession, but can never enable you to hold out when difficult days come. I say it is manifest by this departure from your profession, that some outward self-respect at first allured you to it. As now, when I behold the artificial motions of the wheels in a *watch*, and see how regularly the needle marks the journal-hours of the sun upon the flat of the *quadrant*, and see nothing that moves or guides it; it would cause admiration if I had never seen it before, or did not understand the cause and motion; but when I look upon the other side, and there find wheels, ressorts, and counterpoises, and a spring that causes all those motions, I cease to wonder. Certainly some lust or other was the spring of all thy religious motions; stop or take off that, and motion ceases: And if it be so, this *scab* of hypocrisy will at last break out into that *botch* of apostasy. Thou canst never hold out long under trials, Matt. 13:21. Oh how many such sad sights may we live to see as trials come! Difficult times are coming on, 2 Tim. 3:1. And woe to such then as want sincerity at the bottom of their profession.

2. And as these have no habitual readiness for sufferings, and, consequently, must be ruined by them, so there are others that may be truly godly, and have the root of the matter in them, who are yet far from an actual readiness, and so continuing, are like to be a reproach to religion when their trial comes: for it is not a little grace in the sleepy habit that will secure you from falling scandalously by the hand of temptation: and although that seed of God which is in you will recover you again, and prevent total and final apostasy, yet, Oh, consider what a sad thing it is to enter into, and be conquered by temptation, to be led away in triumph by the tempter, and made a reproach to Christ. O it is a sad consideration to think how many there be amongst the people of God, that discover little or no actual preparations for sufferings: As first,

(1.) Upon how many of the saints is the spirit of slumber poured out? Even the wise, as well as foolish, seem now to be asleep. There is a twofold spiritual sleep, the first is *total*, upon wicked men: and it is one of God's sorest and dreadfullest strokes upon their souls, Isa. 29:10. The

Hebrew word there[1] is the same with that which is used of Adam, when God cast him into that deep sleep whilst he took out his rib. And in 2 Tim. 2:26, it signifies such a sleep as that which is occasioned by drunkenness; out of such a sleep doth the Lord awaken all that are saved, and they never fall into it any more. The other is *partial*, Song of Sol. 5:2, and is incident to the people of God, Matt. 25:5. This is nothing else but the torpor or sluggishness of Spirit which seizeth upon the saints; and never did it prevail, I fear, among them more than now. For where is their activity for God? Where is he that *stirreth up* himself to take hold of God? Isa. 64:7. Where is there such a generation as that, Psa. 24:6? We pray, confer, and hear, for the most part, but, as men speak, betwixt sleeping and waking. Where can you find, except here and there, one that hath a quick and lively sense of God's indignation upon him, or that trembles at his judgments? Is not that the very case of the most which God describes, Isa. 42 *ult*.

(2.) How many are seized by a private and worldly Spirit, every man turning to his own house, and eagerly pursuing the *world*? Hab. 1:9, Jer. 14:4, 5. Oh! how are we entangled in the wilderness? How doth the world eat up our time, and eat out our zeal, cowardize and soften our spirits, and render us utterly unfit for the yoke and burden of Christ? You that see so much beauty, and taste so much sweetness in the creature, you will have an hard task when called to deny it: You are not yet prepared to drink of the cup, or take up the cross of Christ.

(3.) How many poor Christians are of a low and timorous Spirit, ready to tremble at the shaking of a leaf? Ah poor

---

[1] תַּרְדֵּמָה [*tardeimah*]. Αναvηψωσιv [*ananeipsosin*].

hearts! how unfit are you for bonds or death! This passion of fear that so predominates in you, is the very passion which Satan assaults, and lays siege to in the hour of temptation, as was before noted: And commonly it is occasioned (where it flows not from the *natural constitution*) from an excessive love to the world, or some guilt upon the spirit. It is true, the Lord can so assist weak faith, and so subdue strong fears, as that you may be enabled to stand the shock when it comes: (For, as I noted formerly, our strength lies not in anything inherent in us, but we are strong or weak, according to the divine presence and assistances that we enjoy): but yet if you labour not to mortify this evil, and stir not up yourselves in the use of all appointed means, to rouse your zeal and courage for God, I know no warrant you have to expect such assistances.

(4.) *Lastly*, How many poor Christians among us are to this day dark and cloudy in their evidences for heaven? Had they walked closely with God, being laborious in the disquisition and search of their own hearts, they had long since obtained a clearness and satisfaction about the state of their own hearts: But as the case stands with them, how unfit are they for bonds or death. Oh! it is a sad case, when inward and outward troubles meet together, as you may see, Gen. 42:21, when there shall be *fightings without*, and *fears within*: When such a pang as that, Lam. 3:17, 18, shall come over thy heart, what wilt thou do?

By all that hath been said, it appears that the most of professors are in a very unready posture for sufferings; so that as troubles come to an height, we are like to see many sad spectacles: Many offences will come; religion is like to be wounded in the house of its friends. Oh! what a day of mercy have we enjoyed? What helps and choice advantages, above any precedent age, and yet unready? How sad and inexcusable is this?

Chapter 15

Containing another use of the point, by way of exhortation, persuading all the people of God, whilst the Lord respites, and graciously delays their trials, to answer the end of God therein, and prepare themselves for greater trials; where several motives are propounded to excite to the duty.

Up then from your beds of sloth, awake from your security, O ye saints, get upon your watchtowers, tremble in yourselves, that ye may rest in the day of evil, Hab. 2:1, 3, 16. 'Put on the whole armour of God, that ye may be able to stand in the evil day, and when you have done all, to stand,' Eph. 6:11, 13. O let it never be said of your dwellings, as it is said of the tabernacles of the wicked, Job 21:9, 'Their houses are safe from fear.'

Augustus hearing of one that was deeply in debt, who yet slept heartily, sent for his pillow, supposing there was some strange virtue in that pillow. I wonder what pillow ye have gotten, O ye drowsy saints, that you can sleep so quietly upon it, now that all things about you are conspiring trouble, and threatening danger. Can you sleep like Jonah, when seas of wrath are tumbling and roaring round about you, and threaten to entomb you and all your enjoyments? Behold, 'The stork in the heavens knows her appointed time,' Jer. 8:7, and hath not God made you *wiser than the fowls of the air*, Job 35:11. It may be the sound of some present judgment may a little startle you, like a sudden clap of thunder in the air; but how soon doth sloth and security prevail, and overcome you again. They say poison by being habituated, may be made innocent: We are so used to, or rather hardened under calamities, that nothing moves or effectually awakens us. Lord, what will the end of these things be? Wilt thou surprise thy people at unawares? Shall thy judgments find them *secure*, and leave them *desperate*? O that God would persuade you 'to gather yourselves together, yea, to gather together' (not in an unlawful and seditious way, but in the way of duty), 'before the decree bring forth, and the day pass as the chaff,' Zeph. 2:1, 2. O prepare to meet your God, Amos 4:12. Prepare your *faith*, *love*, *courage*, etc., before God call you to the exercise of them.

And to excite you to this duty, besides all the forementioned benefits of a prepared spirit, consider these following particulars by way of motive.

Motive 1. The many calls which God hath given you to this work. The Lord hath uttered his voice, and called from heaven unto you; will you be deaf to his calls? He hath called upon you, (1.) By the word: God would have it cry to you first, because he would give the first honour to his word. He hath given all his prophets *one mouth*, Luke 1:70, and they have warned you faithfully. (2.) By the *rod*: this also hath a loud voice, Mic. 6:9, Psa. 2:5. Men of understanding will hear this voice; and those that will not hear it shall be lashed by it even till they are sick with smiting, Mic. 6:13. (3.) By prodigious and portentous signs in the heavens and earth, such as no age can parallel, these have a loud voice to all that regard the works of the Lord, or the operations of his hands. Eusebius calls them *God's sermons to the world*.[1] O that we were wise to consider what God's ends are in these things! one observes, 'That as they are the plainest and most obvious to sense, so they are commonly the last sermons which God intends to preach to nations, before he inflicts his punishment on them, if they repent not.' O let not God, speaking in ordinary and extraordinary ways to you, still speak in vain.

Your preparations for sufferings are the most probable means of preventing your fall and ruin by those sufferings.

Motive 2. Sufferings prove fatal and destructive to some; but it is to secure and careless ones; Such as are diligent and faithful in the use of God's means, are secured from the danger. Christ lays our constancy and perseverance very much upon our forecasting the worst that may fall out, Luke 14:28. 'Put on the whole armour of God, that ye may be able to stand,' Eph. 6:11. He that hath first severed Christ in his thoughts from all worldly advantages, and puts the case thus to his own soul, O my soul, canst thou embrace or love a naked Christ? Canst thou be content to be impoverished, imprisoned, and suffer the loss of all for him? He is most likely to cleave faithfully to him, when the case is really presented to him indeed. And can it seem a light thing in your eyes, to be enabled to stand in such an evil day? If you fall away from Christ, then all you have wrought is lost, Ezek. 33:13. Gideon's one *bastard* destroyed all his seventy sons. This act renders all former actions and

[1] *Euseb. hist. lib*. iii. cap. 8.

professions vain. If you fall, you shall thereby be brought into a more perfect bondage to the devil than ever, Matt. 12:45. Yea, ordinarily, apostates are judicially given up to be persecutors, Hos. 5:12, 1 Tim. 1:20, and are seldom or never recovered again by grace, Heb. 6:4, 6. They that lick up their vomit, seldom cast it up any more. It is a fall within a little as low as the unpardonable sin, whence never any rise again. In some cases the *judge* will not allow the *offender* his book. And is it not then a choice and desirable mercy to escape and prevent such a fall as this? O good souls, ply your preparation-work close then; prepare, or you perish.

Motive 3. This will best answer the grace of God, in affording you such choice helps and advantages as you have enjoyed. How long have you enjoyed the free liberty of the gospel, shining in its lustre among you? This sun, which to some other nations hath not risen, and to divers on whom it hath shined, yet it is but as a winter's sun, remote, and its beams but feeble; but you have lived, as it were, under the *line*, it hath been over your heads, and shed its richest influences upon you. Yea, God's ministers, who are not only appointed to be *watchmen*, Ezek. 3:17, but *trumpeters* to discover danger, Num. 10:8. These have faithfully warned you of a day of trouble, and given you their best assistance to make you ready for it. And is not their joy, yea, life, bound up in your stability in such a day of trial? Doth not everyone call upon you in the words of the apostle, Phil. 4:1, 'Therefore, my brethren, dearly beloved and longed for, my joy and crown, so stand fast in the Lord, my dearly beloved.' Will it not cut them to the very heart, if after all their spending labours among you, they still leave you unready? enemies still to the cross of Christ, impossible to be reconciled and persuaded to suffering-work for Christ.

I remember I have read of the Athenian Codrus, who being informed by the *oracle*, that the people whose king should be slain in battle should be conquerors: he thereupon disrobed himself, and in a disguise went into the enemies quarters, that he might steal a death to make his people victorious.

Oh! how glad would your ministers be, if you might conquer and overcome in the day of temptation, whatever become of their lives and liberties! *Yea, and if they be offered up upon the sacrifice and service of your faith, they can rejoice, and joy with you all.* Such is their zeal and longing after your security and welfare. But if still you remain an unready people, and do become a prey to temptation, Oh how inexcusable will you be!

Motive 4. Remember how ready the Lord Jesus was to suffer the hardest and vilest things for you. He had a bitter cup put into his hands to drink for you, into which the wrath both of God and man was squeezed out. Never had man such sufferings to undergo as Christ,[1] whether you consider, (1.) The dignity of his person, who was in the form of God, and might have stood upon his *peerage* and equality with him; he is the *sparkling diamond of heaven*, Acts 7:56, the *darling* of the Father's soul, Isa. 42:1, *glorious* as the only begotten of the Father, John 1:14, yea, *glory* itself, James 2:1, yea, the very *brightness of glory*, Heb. 1:8. He is

---

[1] *Dolor Christi fuit major omnibus doloribus.* Aquinas. 'The suffering of Christ was greater than all other sufferings.'

the *deliciae Christiani orbis*,[1] *fairer than the sons of men*; And for him to be so debased, below so many thousands of his own creatures, *become a worm, and no man*; this was a wonderful humiliation. It was Jeremiah's lamentation, that such as were brought up in scarlet, embraced dunghills; that princes were hanged up by the hands, and the faces of elders were not reverenced: But what was that to the humiliation of the Lord of glory? Or, (2.) That he suffered in the prime and flower of his years; when full of life and sense, and more capable of exquisite sense of pain than others: for he was *optime complexionatus*,[2] of a singular constitution; and all the while he hanged on the tree, his sense of pain not at all blunted or decayed, Mark 15:37, 39. Or, (3.) The manner of his death. It was the death of the cross, which was a *rack* to Christ: for in reference to the distention of his members upon the cross is that spoken, Psa. 22:17, 'I may tell all my bones.' Or, (4.) That all this while God hid his face from him. When Stephen suffered, he saw the heavens opened. The *martyrs* were many of them ravished and transported with ecstasies of joy in their sufferings; but Christ in the dark. He suffered in his soul as well as in his body; and the sufferings of his soul were the very soul of his sufferings. It was the Father's wrath that lay so heavy on him, as to put him into such an agony, that an instance was never given of the like nature: for he sweat θρόμβοι [*thromboi*], great drops, or clodders of blood, which fell from his body to the ground, Luke 22:44.[3] 'It amazed him,

---

[1] 'the darling of the Christian world.'

[2] Aquinas.

[3] While sweating blood appears to be a rare condition that can occur, the Greek uses the comparative particle ὡσεί (*hosei; like*)

and made him very heavy'; see Mark 14:33, yea, 'sorrowful even to death,' Matt. 26:38.

And yet, as bitter as the cup was, he freely and willingly drank it up, John 18:11, prepared himself to be offered up a sacrifice, Psa. 40:6, 7, 'gave his back to the smiters,' Isa. 50:6, yea, longed exceedingly for the time till it came, Luke 12:50.

Now, if Christ so cheerfully prepared and addressed himself to such sufferings as these for you, should you not prepare yourselves to encounter any *difficulty* or *hardships* for him? O my brethren, doth not this seem a just and fair inference to you, from the sufferings of Christ for you? 1 Pet. 4:1, 'Forasmuch then as Christ hath suffered for us in the flesh, arm yourselves likewise with the same mind.'

Oh, trifle no longer, feed not yourselves with fancies and groundless presumptions of immunity and peace, but foresee difficulties, and fit yourselves to bear them.

---

which does not indicate Christ actually sweated blood, simply that his sweat was similar to blood—P.

Chapter 16

Containing the last use of the point, by way of support and comfort to poor trembling souls, who do take pains to make themselves ready for sufferings; but yet finding such strength in Satan's temptations, and their own corruptions, fear that all their labour is vain, and that they shall faint, and utterly apostatize, when their troubles and trials come to an height.

In the last place, if it be such a blessed thing to be ready for bonds, or death for Christ, this may minister much comfort to such souls, who though they cannot say as Paul here did, that they are ready; yet are at work daily upon their own hearts to make them ready, and strive, in the use of all means, to *conquer* those corruptions that hinder it, and improve those graces in which it mainly consisteth. O poor soul, whatever present unreadiness or indisposition thou findest, and complainest of in thine heart, yet thy condition is safe.

Objection. Oh! but I cannot be satisfied in that: I fear I shall be overborne by temptations when they come to an height. I have such experience of the deceits and treacherousness of my own heart, that it seems impossible to me to do as these blessed souls did, when I come to the like trials.

Solution. It is well thou suspectest thine own heart, and tremblest in thyself; this fear will keep thee waking, while others are securely sleeping. It was a good saying of a reverend minister, now with God, 'He that fears to flinch, shall never flinch for fear.' It is true, seeming grace may be totally lost, Luke 8:18, Heb. 6:4, 5, 2 Pet. 2:20. It is granted also, that the sin of believers deserve that God should forsake them, and that he may suffer grace in them to be sadly abated, and they may fall before a temptation, as Peter, and all the disciples did: but that thou shalt never be separated from Christ, or fall *totus a toto, in totum*, utterly away from God, thou mayest be abundantly satisfied, upon these five or six grounds.

1. From God's eternal electing love, wherewithal gracious souls are beloved and embraced, be their graces never so weak, or their corruptions never so strong. This is immutable, Heb. 6:18, and hence it is said, Mark 13:22, 'They shall deceive (if it were possible) the very elect.' Now, this immutable purpose of God, is not founded upon any mutable ground or reason in thee, Rom. 9:11. Yea, when he, Rom. 8:29, elected thee, he saw what thou wouldst be, and yet that hindered him not.

2. From the covenant of grace, in the bosom of which thou art wrapped up: this is all thy salvation, and all thy hope; it will afford thee abundant satisfaction, if thou do but weigh particularly these three things about it. (i) That the Author of this covenant is not a *fickle* creature, but a *faithful* God, with whom there is not *yea* and *nay*; with whom *there is no variableness, nor shadow of turning*; whose gifts and callings are without repentance; so that once within this blessed covenant, and in it forever. (ii) That God hath established the covenant with you in the blood of Christ;

therefore the *sacramental cup*, is called 'the cup of the New Testament in his blood,' Luke 22:20. The everlasting merit and efficacy whereof gives the soul of a believer the highest satisfaction imaginable. (iii) *Lastly*, Add to this, that in this covenant God hath undertaken for us, as well as for himself: so that what is a *condition* in one scripture, is the matter of a *promise* in another, Jer. 32:40.

3. From that strict and intimate union that is betwixt Christ and thee. And hence it is impossible thou shouldst be lost. For, (i) Thy union with his person brings interest in his properties along with it. Whatever he is, or hath, it is for thee: his eye of knowledge, arm of power, bowels of pity, it is all for thee. (ii) This union with his person, secures thy feeble graces from perishing, John 4:14. Thy graces have an everlasting spring. Whilst there is sap in this root, it will ascend into the branches. (iii) It implies thy perseverance, because by this union thou becomest an integral part of Christ's body, which would be mutilated and defective, should thou be *cut* off and lost.

4. From the prevalent intercession of Jesus Christ in the heavens, for all his saints, in all their trials here on earth. From hence the apostle infers the certainty of our perseverance, Rom. 8:34, and a pregnant instance of it you have in Peter's case, Luke 22:32. So Heb. 7:25 speaks fully to the case. To strengthen this, consider, (i) Who it is that intercedes: It is Christ, whose person is most dear and ingratiated with the Father, John 11:42. (ii) What he intercedes for: Surely for nothing but, what is most suitable to his Father's will. The will of Christ's and his Father's do not clash, John 16:26, 27, yea, what he prays for, he prays not for *gratis*, or asks upon

any dishonourable terms to the justice of his Father; but they are all mercies purchased and paid for; and therefore fear not the failing of your graces.

5. From the Spirit of Christ which dwelleth and abideth in thee, and hath begun his saving work upon thee. I say, *saving*, for else it would afford no argument. His common works on hypocrites come to nothing, but in thee they cannot fail. For, (i) His honour is pledged and engaged to perfect it. That reproach of the foolish builder shall never lie upon him, that he began to build, but could not finish. Besides, this would make void all that the Father and the Son have done for thee; both their works are complete and perfect in their kinds, and the Spirit is the last efficient in order of working. (ii) Besides, the grace he hath already wrought in thee, may give thee yet further and fuller assurance of its preservation, inasmuch as it hath the nature of a *seal*, *pledge*, and *earnest* of the whole, Rom. 8:23, 2 Cor. 1:22. So that it cannot fail.

6. From those multitudes of *assertory*, *promissory*, and *comparative* scriptures, the rich veins whereof run through the book of God, as so many streams to refresh thy soul. Of *assertory* scriptures, see John 6:39, John 10:28, 1 John 2:19. Of *promissory* scriptures, see Isa. 54:10, Jer. 32:40, 1 Cor. 1:8, etc. Of *comparative* scriptures, see Psa. 1:3, Psa. 125, 1 John 4:14, etc. The principal scope of all which is to shew the indefectible nature of true grace in the saints.

And now, how should this refresh thy drooping soul, make thee gird up the loins of thy mind, since thou dost 'not run as one uncertain, neither fightest as one that beats the air,' 1 Cor. 9:26, but art so secured from total apostasy, as thou seest thou art by all these things. O bless ye the Lord.

Objection. 2. But the Lord seems to be departed from my soul; God is afar off from me; and troubles are near. I seem to be in such a case as Saul was when the Philistines made war upon him, and God was departed from him; and therefore I shall fall.

Solution. Not so; for there are two sorts of divine desertions; the one is *absolute*, when the Lord utterly forsakes his creatures, so that they shall never behold his face more: The other is *limited* and *respective*, and so he forsook his own Son, and often does his own *elect*: and of this kind, some are only *cautional*, to prevent sin; some are merely *probational*, to try grace; and others *castigatory*, to chastise our negligence and carelessness. Now, though I have not a word of comfort to speak in the case of total and absolute desertions; yet of the latter (which doubtless is thy case) much may be said by way of support, be it of which of the three sorts it will, or in what degree it will. For,

1. This hath been the case of many precious souls, Psa. 22:1, 2, Psa. 77:2, Psa. 88:9, Job 13:24-26. This was poor Mr Glover's case, as you will find in his story, and it continued till he came within sight of the stake;[1] therefore no new or strange thing hath happened unto you.

2. The Lord by this will advantage thee for perseverance, not only as they are cautioned against sin, but as they make thee hold Christ the faster, and prize his presence at an

---

[1] Robert Glover was an English Protestant martyr who was burnt at Coventry in September 1555.

higher rate, when he shall please graciously to manifest himself to thee again, Song of Sol. 3:4.

3. This shall not abide forever: it is but a little cloud, and will blow over. It is but for a *moment*, and that moment's darkness ushers in everlasting light, Isa. 54:7.

4. Yea, *lastly*, The light of God's countenance shall not only be restored *certainly*, but it shall be restored *seasonably*; when the darkness is *greatest*, thy troubles at the *highest*, and thy hopes *lowest*. He is a God of judgment, and knows how to time his own mercies, Psa. 138:3.

Objection. 3. But I am a weak woman, or a young person, how shall I be able to confess Christ before rulers, and look great ones in the face?

Solution. 1. Christ delights to make his power known in such, 2 Cor. 12:9, for he affects not social glory.

2. 'Thou shalt be holden up, for God is able to make thee stand,' Rom. 14:4. Thou that art sensible of thine own infirmity, mayest run to that promise.

3. Such poor weak creatures shall endure when stronger (if self-confident) fall, Isa. 40:30, 31, 'Even the youths shall faint and be weary, and the young men utterly fall. But they that wait upon the Lord, shall renew their strength; they shall mount up with wings as eagles, run and not be weary, walk and not faint.'

Youths, and young men, are bold, daring, and confident persons, that trust to their own strength; to whom such as wait upon the Lord stand here opposed; they shall faint, but these shall renew their strength.

Art thou one that waitest and dependest upon an all-sufficient God, in the sense of thine own weakness? This promise then is for thee.

4. You may furnish yourselves at pleasure, with examples of the mighty power of God resting upon such as you are, out of our own martyrology.

Thomas Drowry the poor blind boy (Fox, vol. 3. p. 703). What a presence of spirit was with him, when examined by the Chancellor!

Eulalia, a virgin of about twelve years of age, see how she acted above those years, yea, above the power of nature (Fox, vol. 1. p. 120). Tender women, yea, children, act above themselves, when assisted by a strong God.

And thus you have some help offered you by a weak hand, in your present and most important work.

The Lord carry home all with power upon your hearts, that if God call you to suffer for him, you may say as Paul did, 'I am now ready to be offered up, and the time of my departure is at hand. I have fought a good fight, I have finished my course, l have kept the faith: henceforth there is laid up for me a crown of righteousness, which God the righteous Judge shall give me at that day: and not to me only, but to them also which love his appearing,' 2 Tim. 4:6-8. And as you expect so to finish your course with joy; be diligent in the use of all means, to prepare and make yourselves ready to follow the call of God, whether it be to bonds, or to death, for the name of the Lord Jesus.

———

PURITAN 🐏 PAPERBACKS

PURITAN PAPERBACKS

BANNER *of* **TRUTH**

THE Banner of Truth Trust originated in 1957 in London. The founders believed that much of the best literature of historic Christianity had been allowed to fall into oblivion and that, under God, its recovery could well lead not only to a strengthening of the church, but to true revival.

Inter-denominational in vision, this publishing work is now international, and our lists include a number of contemporary authors along with classics from the past. The translation of these books into many languages is encouraged.

A monthly magazine, *The Banner of Truth*, is also published. More information about this and all our publications can be found on our website or supplied by either of the offices below.

Head Office:
3 Murrayfield Road
Edinburgh
EH12 6EL
United Kingdom
Email: info@banneroftruth.co.uk

North America Office:
PO Box 621
Carlisle, PA 17013
United States of America
Email: info@banneroftruth.org